BINCHE LACE

BINCHE LACE

MICHAEL GIUSIANA
WITH
LINDA DUNN

Graphics by Brenda Lispcomb

Dryad Press Ltd, London

Acknowledgement

I have been fortunate to have had the opportunity to study lacemaking with Barbara Holderness, Brigita Fuhrman, Anna Blanco, Doris Southard, Mary McPeek, Mevr Neyrinck and Annamarie Verbeke-Billiet, and, for the past six years, to work and study with Susanne Van Ruymbeke. To these women I am indebted. This book was written with the hope that it will assist other lacemakers in the same way that my teachers have helped and assisted me.

I want to say thank you to all those who encouraged me from the start, and to all those who have assisted me throughout this project. A very special thank you to Puck, and Brenda, and to Susan and Bill who helped me keep it all together.

© Michael Giusiana 1989
First published in 1989

ISBN 0 8521 9810 8

Set in Monophoto Old Style
Typeset by Keyspools Ltd, Golborne, Lancs.
and printed in Great Britain by
Bath Press, Bath
for the Publishers
Dryad Press Ltd
8 Cavendish Square
London W1M 0AJ

A CIP record for this book is available from the
British Library

Contents

Introduction

This book is designed to provide a basic introduction to working Binche lace: no history is given. The aim of this book is purely to offer 'how-to' knowledge. It is written for those lacemakers who work from coloured diagrams, and is divided into three main sections.

The first section is a photographic review of Flanders, Point de Paris, Valenciennes and Binche laces. It offers an overview of the basic stitches used in these laces using both colour and line diagrams. The sample pieces are worked with 100/3 cotton with the exception of the Valenciennes grounds, which are worked in 140 Egyptian Cotton.

The second section describes the snowflakes which provide the foundation for the fillings or grounds used in Binche lace. The sample pieces offer the lacemaker an opportunity to understand not only how to work the lace, but also how it is constructed. All samples in this section are worked with Brok 100/3 cotton.

The third section offers a selection of Binche patterns based upon antique laces and diagrams from old teaching manuals. A variety of threads are used in this section.

It is recommended that the pieces be worked sequentially, starting with the Flanders ground and continuing through the snowflakes, before you begin the patternwork. If you chose to do the pattern work only, the beginning sections should provide assistance in the basic techniques of Binche.

Binche Lace: erratum

K ey to diagrams

Black lines represent stitches worked in *whole stitch and twist:* cross, twist, cross, twist (see note on prickings, p. 68).

Blue lines with black dots represent stitches worked in *half stitch*: cross, twist.

Medium blue lines represent stitches worked in *linen stitch* (also known as *whole stitch* or *cloth stitch*): cross, twist, cross.

Thick blue lines represent *braids*: cross, twist, cross, twist, etc.

⊤ Indicates the start of a new pair.

⊥ Indicates the end of a pair.

Slash mark on diagrams indicate twists additional to whole stitch and twist.
     In the pattern section starting on p. 68, the only twists indicated are those unique to that particular piece; the normal twists for snowflakes are not shown.

 Schematic drawings are used on page 27, and repeated again on pages 28 and 29 to illustrate the ground stitch for Valenciennes lace. In these drawings one black line represents one thread, not a pair of threads. An example of a braid (plait) is shown.

p. 53 Black dots on black lines should be black dots on blue lines
p. 62–3 Black lines should be blue and vice versa
p. 65 Black lines should be blue.

Key to diagrams

Blue lines represent stitches worked in *whole stitch*: cross, twist, cross, twist.

Thin black lines with blue dots represent stitches worked in *half stitch*: cross, twist.

Medium black lines represent stitches worked in *linen stitch*: cross, twist, cross.

Thick black lines represent *braids*: cross, twist, cross, twist, etc.

Indicates the start of a new pair.

Indicates the end of a pair.

Slash mark on diagrams indicate additional twists. It is understood that a pair finishing a linen stitch is twisted before it begins either a whole stitch or a half stitch. In the pattern section, the only twists indicated are those unique to that particular piece. The normal twists for snowflakes are not shown.

Schematic drawings are used on page 27, and repeated again on pages 28 and 29 to illustrate the stitchwork for Valenciennes lace. In these drawings one black line represents one thread, not a pair of threads. An example of a braid is shown.

Flanders lace

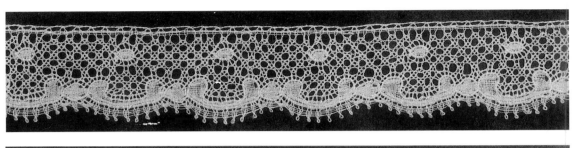

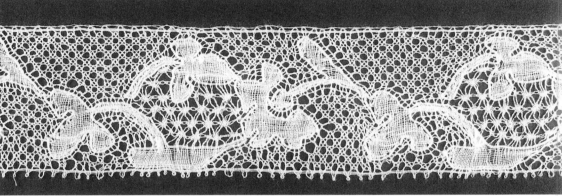

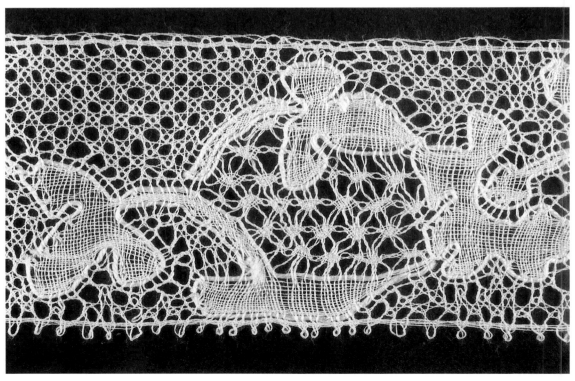

Top: Flanders lace, actual size (2.5 cm)   **Above:** Flanders lace, actual size (3.6 cm)
Below: Detail of the above lace

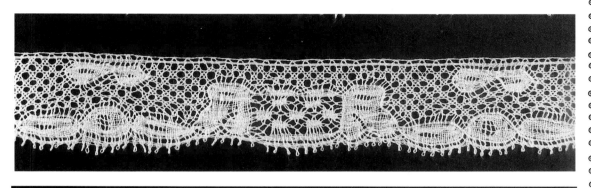

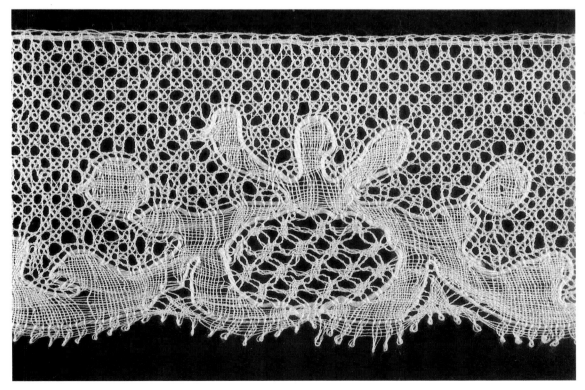

Top: Flanders lace, actual size (2.4 cm) **Above:** Flanders lace, actual size (5 cm)
Below: Detail of the above lace

9

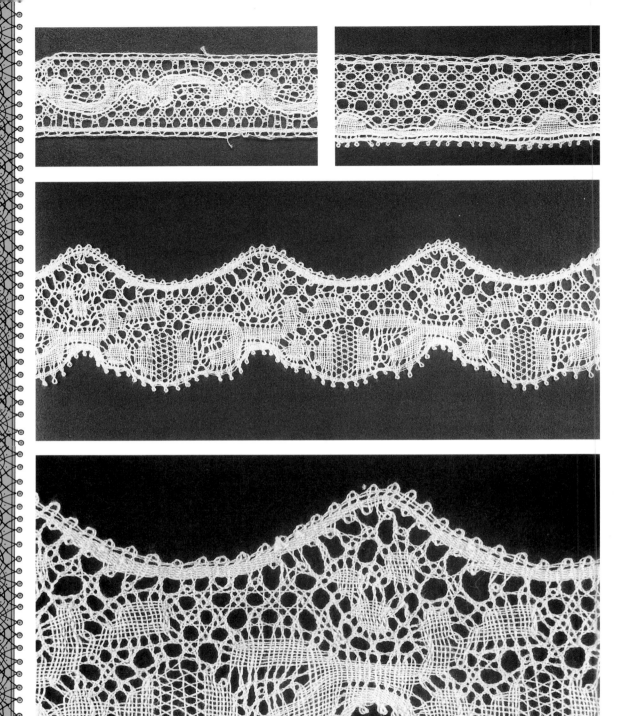

Top left: Flanders lace, actual size (2.1 cm)   **Top right:** Flanders lace, actual size (2.1 cm)
Above: Flanders lace, actual size (2.5 cm)   **Below:** Detail of the above lace

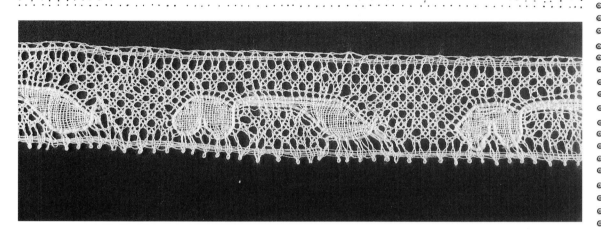

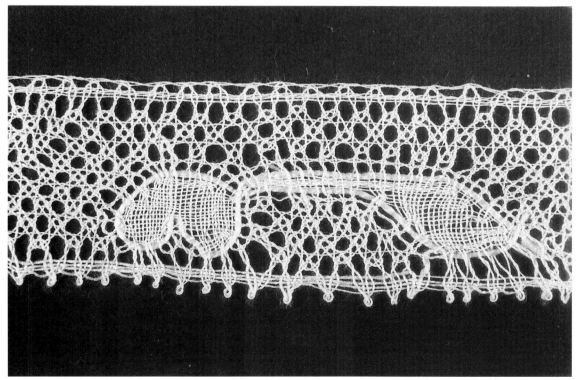

Top: Flanders pricking, reduced 80% from original actual size (2.4 cm) **Above:** Flanders lace, **Below:** Detail of the above lace

Flanders grounds

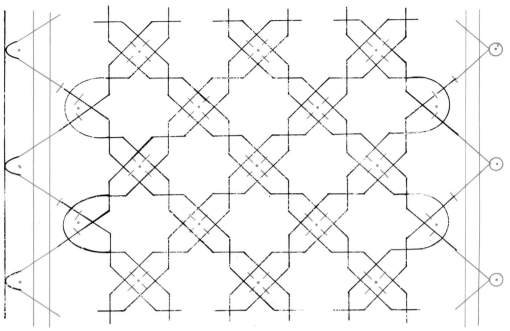

Above: Flanders ground 1   **Below:** (from left to right) Flanders prickings, Flanders ground 1, Flanders ground 2, and Flanders ground 3. Bobbins required: 38

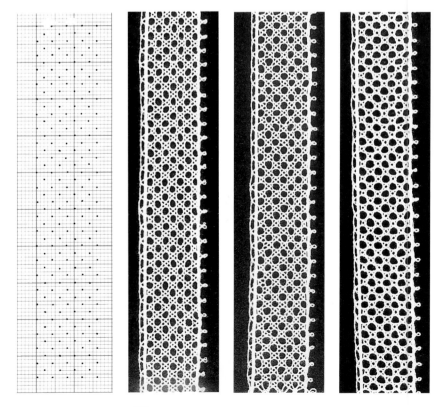

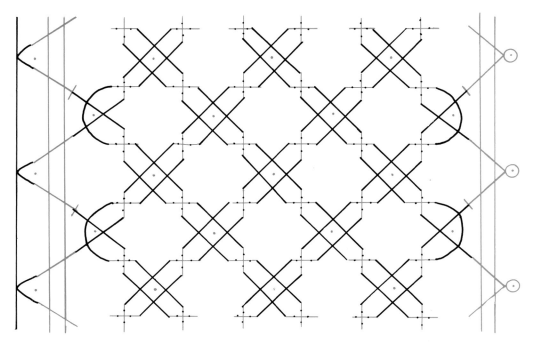

Top: Flanders ground 2   **Below:** Flanders ground 3

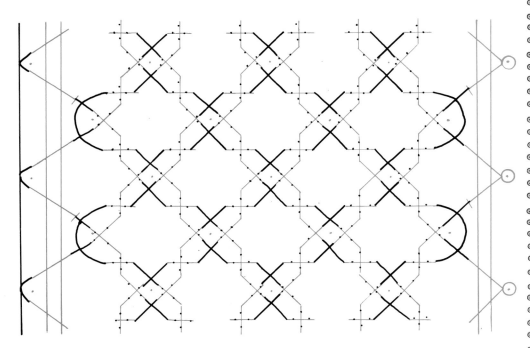

Flanders grounds

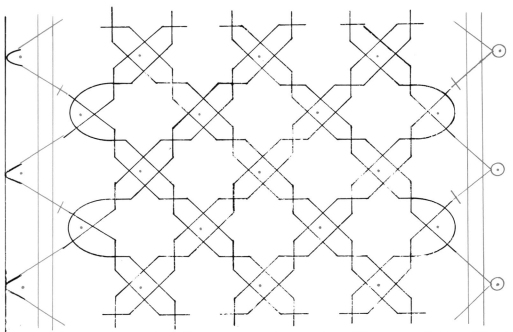

Above: Flanders ground 4 **Below:** (from left to right) Flanders pricking, Flanders ground 4, Flanders ground 5 and Flanders ground 6. Bobbins required: 38

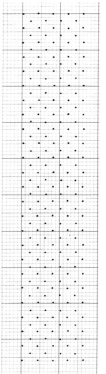

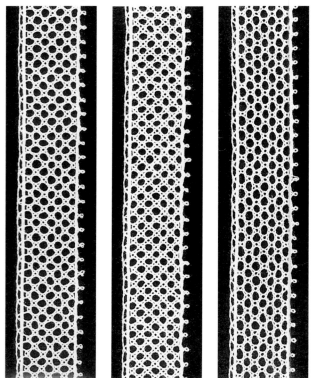

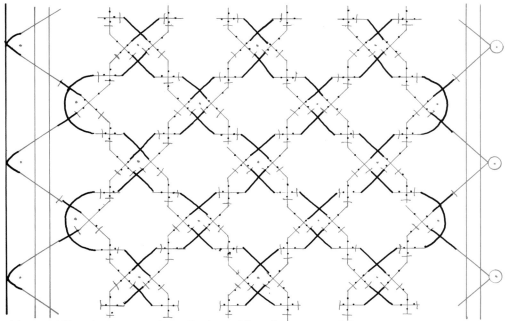

Above: Flanders ground 5   **Below:** Flanders ground 6

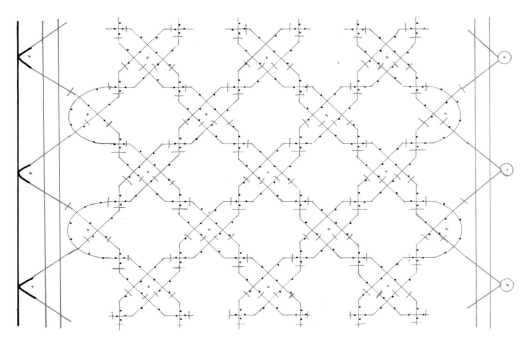

Point de Paris

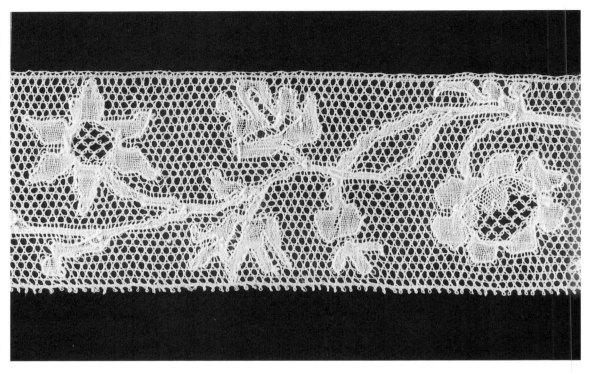

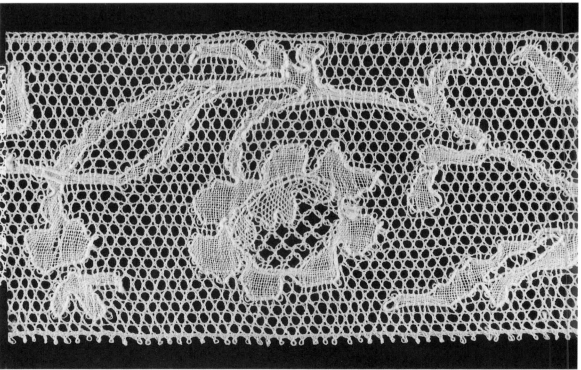

Above: Point de Paris, actual size (6.9 cm)   **Below:** Detail of the above lace

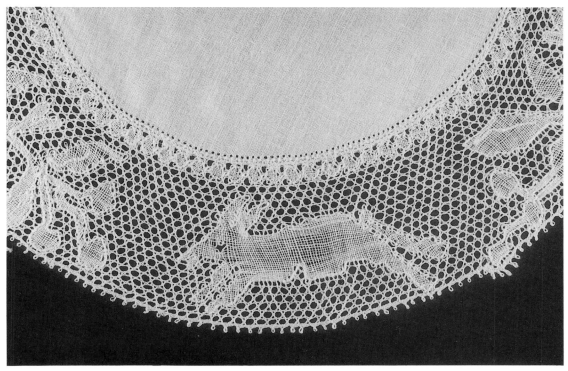

Above: Point de Paris, actual size (22 cm)   **Below:** Detail of the above lace

Above left: Point de Paris mat, reduced (original size 16 cm in diameter) **Below left:**
Detail of the above lace **Above:** Point de Paris pricking

Point de Paris grid

When working out Belgium laces, a given angle for each lace, as in Bucks Point, is not used; instead a ratio of horizontal units to vertical units is used to construct the correct grid. Although this ratio allows the corresponding angle to be determined, this is not done for the Belgium laces.

The ratio of Point de Paris is 6 to 10. To construct the correct grid, the lacemaker measures off a 2.6 cm square. Across the top and bottom the lacemaker then divides the horizontal edge into six equal parts. The next step is to divide the vertical edges into 10 equal parts (top right).

After dividing each of the four sides of the square, diagonal lines are drawn to connect the divisions. This will form a diamond-shaped grid (centre right).

After the diagonals are drawn, a black dot, representing a pinhole, is placed at the points where the diagonals cross one another. Once this is done the lacemaker will have an accurate pricking for Paris ground.

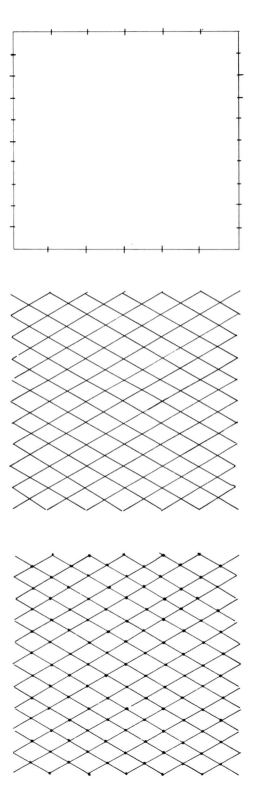

Point de Paris ground

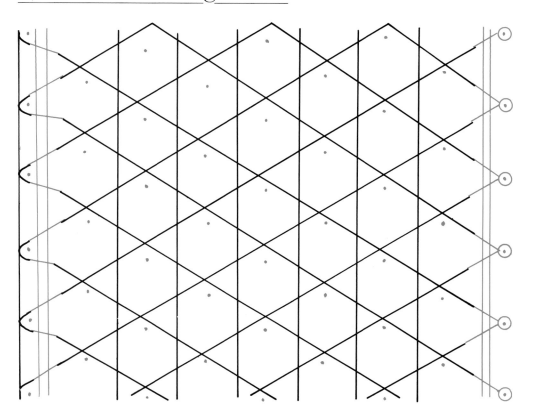

Above: Paris ground   **Below:** (from right to left) Paris ground, and Paris pricking. Bobbins required: 36

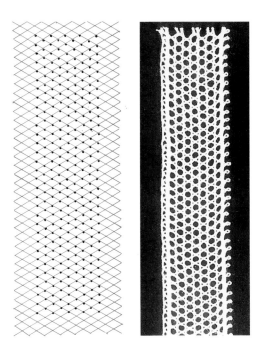

Valenciennes lace

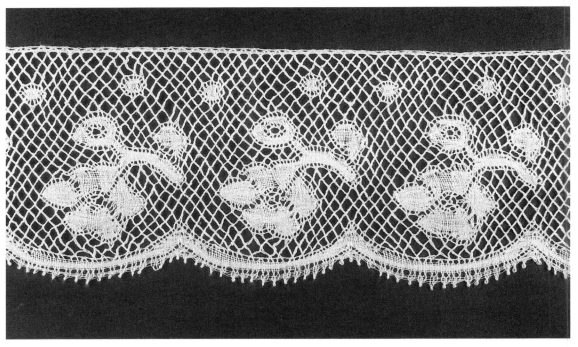

Above: Valenciennes lace; diamond mesh, actual size (6 cm)
Below: Detail of the above lace

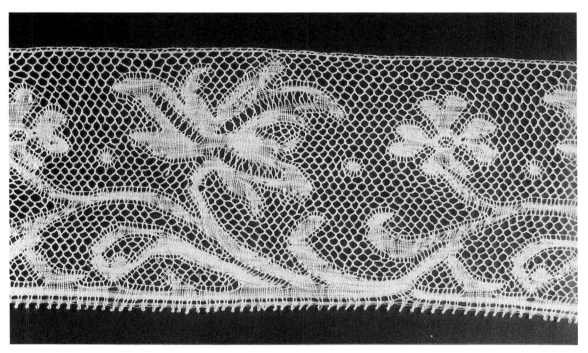

Above: Valenciennes lace, round mesh, actual size (6.5 cm)
Below: Detail of the above lace

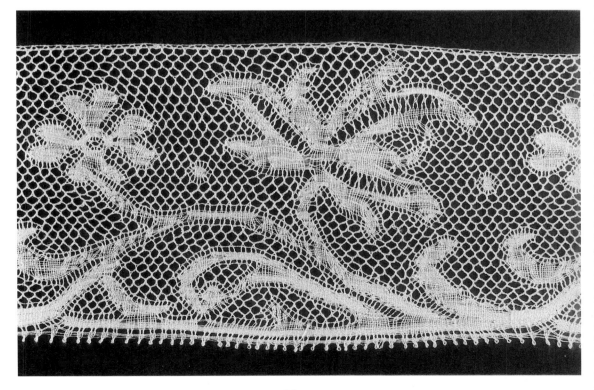

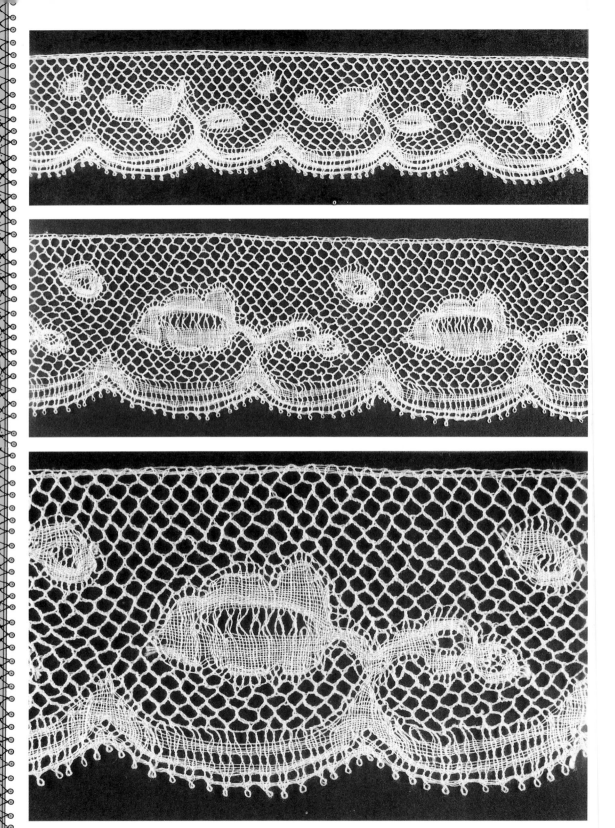

Top: Valenciennes lace, round mesh, actual size (3 cm)   **Above:** Valenciennes lace, round mesh, actual size (4.5 cm)   **Below:** Detail of the above lace

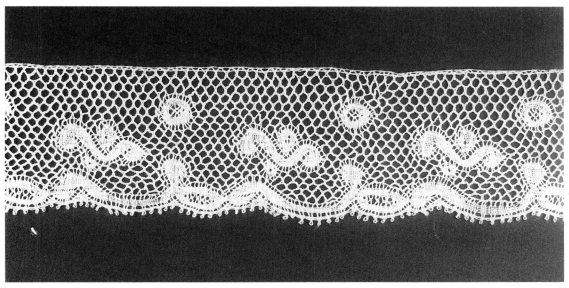

Top: Valenciennes lace, diamond mesh, actual size (2.5 cm)   **Above:** Valenciennes lace, round mesh, actual size (3.2 cm)   **Below:** Valenciennes prickings

Valenciennes grid

The ratio of horizontal to vertical units used in constructing the grid for Valenciennes lace is 8 to 10. To draw the appropriate grid for a fine Valenciennes lace, the initial square should be 2.3 cm wide. Such a fine grid is rarely used, however. For a coarse Valenciennes grid, the width of the initial square would be 3 cm.

Valenciennes lace does not use pins to support the ground. Pins are used only to support the motif. To make the pricking, pinholes are placed at the points at which the diagonals cross. The pinholes are placed in a straight vertical line.

Below are three of the most common grid sizes: 2.5 cm, 2.8 cm and 3 cm. It is possible to purchase commercially prepared grids in these sizes.

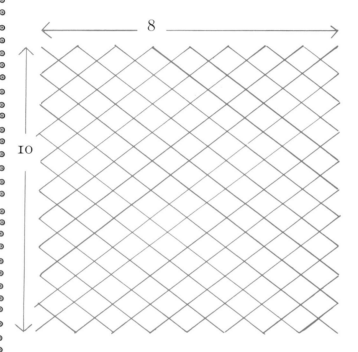

2.5 cm   2.8 cm   3.0 cm

Valenciennes diagrams

```
        c,t,c,t                              c,t,c,t
     c,t        c,t                      (t)         (t)
     c,t        c,t                  c,t,c,t              c,t,c,t
     c,t        c,t                      (t)               (t)
     c,t        c,t                  c,t,c,t              c,t,c,t
                                         (t)                 (t)
```

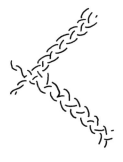

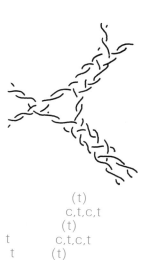

```
            c,t                              (t)
            c,t                          c,t,c,t
 t,         c,t                              (t)
   t,       c,t                   t       c,t,c,t
     c,t,c,t                      t           (t)
     t      c,t                      c,t,c,t    t
            c,t                      t      (t)
              c,t                         c,t,c,t
                c,t                          (t)
```

Top left: Schematic drawing of diamond mesh **Top right:** Schematic drawing of round mesh illustrated through the use of abbreviations: c = cross, t = twist, (t) = twist both pairs **Centre left:** Schematic drawing of diamond mesh ground **Bottom left:** Schematic drawing of diamond mesh connection **Bottom right:** Schematic drawing of round mesh connection. Both connections are reversed for the picot edge

Diamond mesh

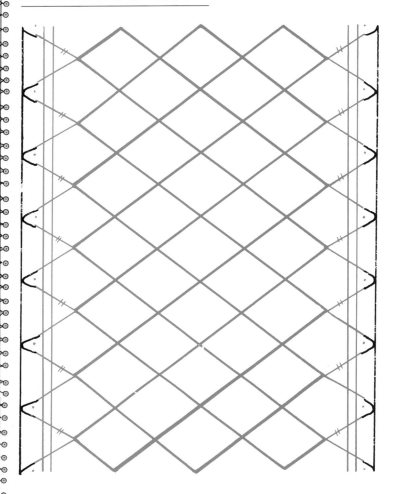

Above: Valenciennes, diamond
mesh   **Below:** (from left to right)
Schematic diagram, pricking, and diamond
mesh ground. Bobbins required: 40

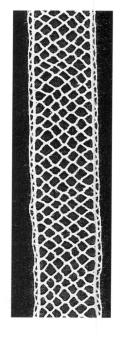

Round mesh

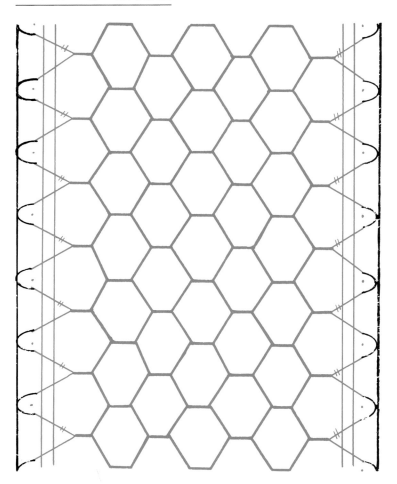

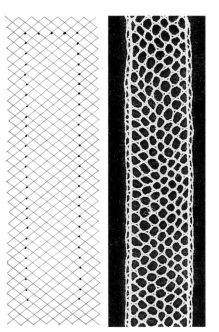

Above: Valenciennes, round mesh **Below:** (from left to right) Round mesh ground, pricking, and schematic diagram. Bobbins required: 40

Binche lace

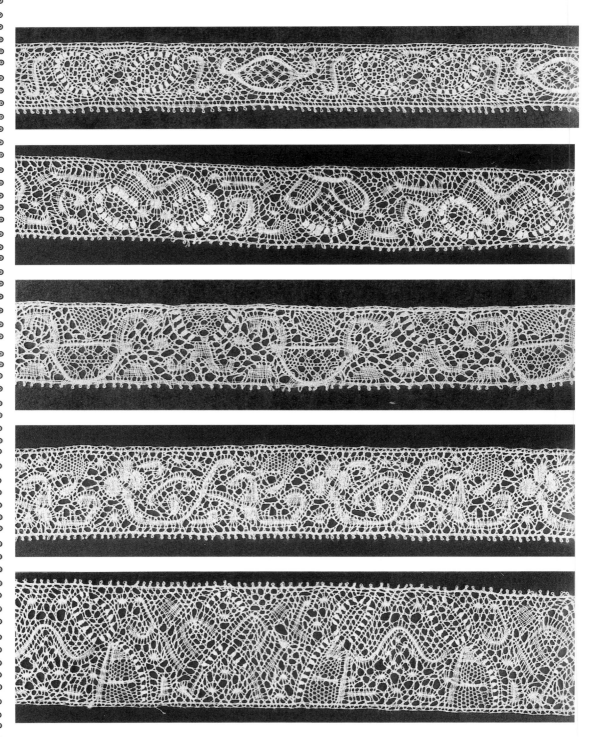

Above: (from top to bottom) Binche lace: 'the fish', actual size (1.7 cm); 'the brill' or 'the eyeglass', actual size (1.9 cm); '13th century' or 'the helmet', actual size (2 cm); Binche lace, name unknown, actual size (2.2 cm); and 'the adoration', actual size (2.7 cm)

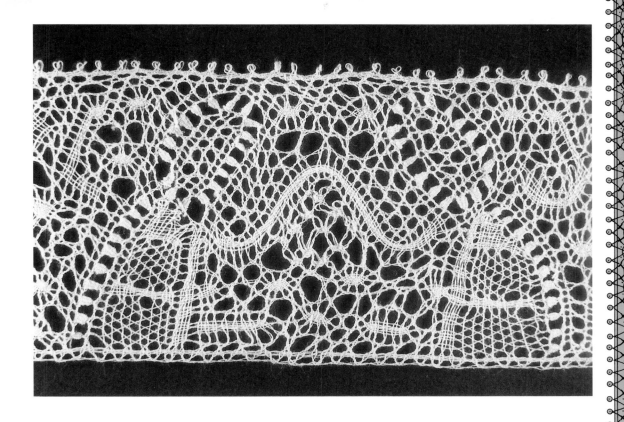

Above and below: Details of 'the adoration'

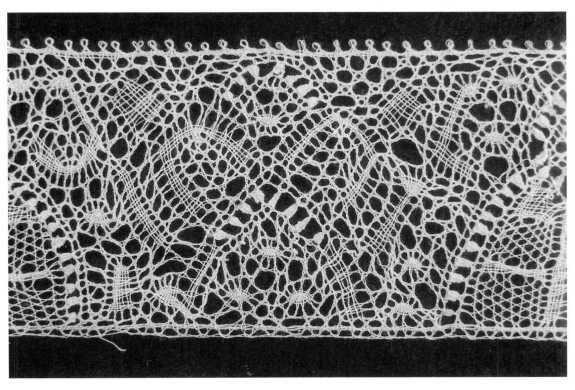

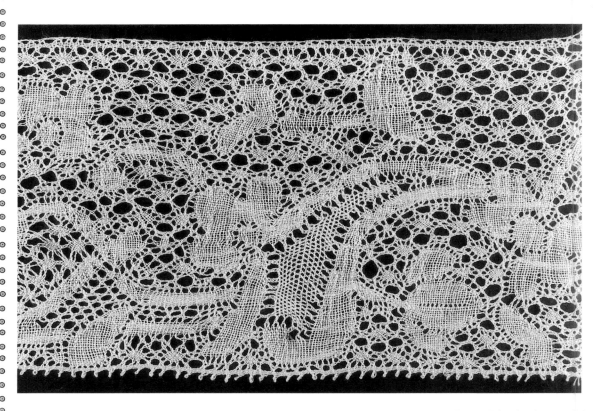

Above: Binche lace, actual size (8.7 cm)   **Below:** Detail of the above lace. Binche lace with half stitch areas such as these are classified as 'mentebolle work'

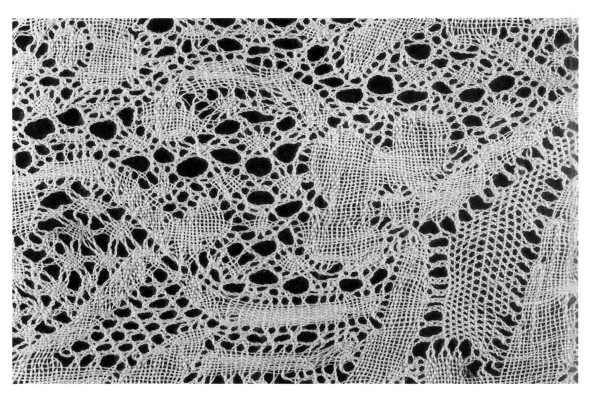

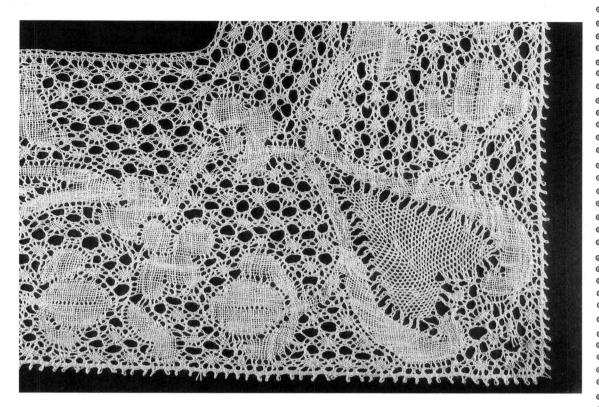

Above: Binche lace, actual size (8.7 cm). This is the corner for the lace on the facing page
Below: Binche lace, reduced (original size 12.2 cm in diameter)

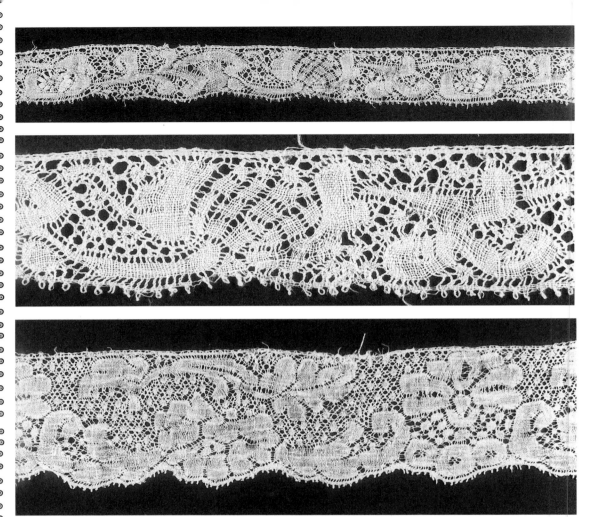
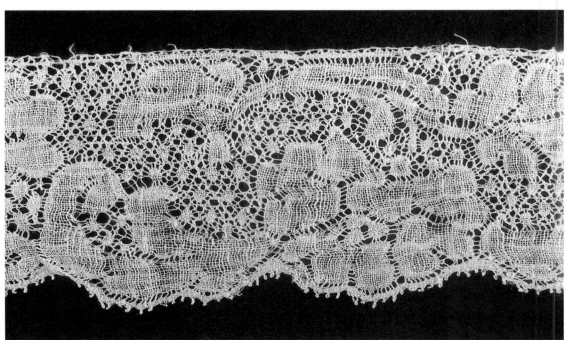

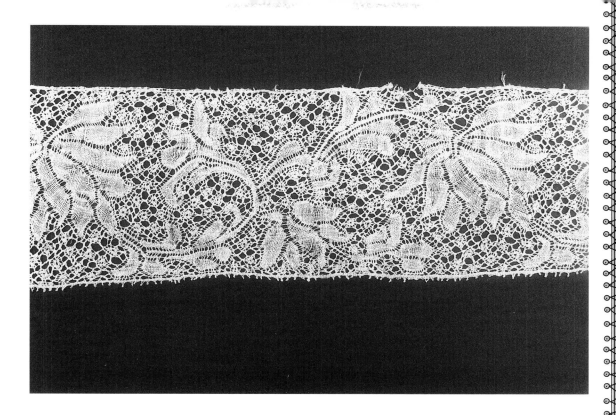

Left: (from top to bottom) Binche lace, actual size (1.2 cm); detail of the above lace; Binche lace, actual size (3.4 cm); detail of the above lace   **Above:** Binche lace, atual size (4.6 cm)
Below: Detail of the above lace

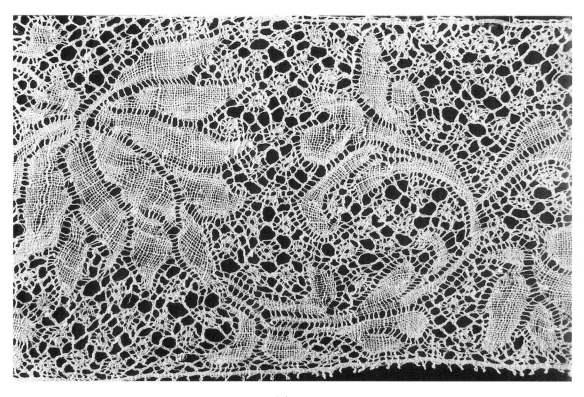

35

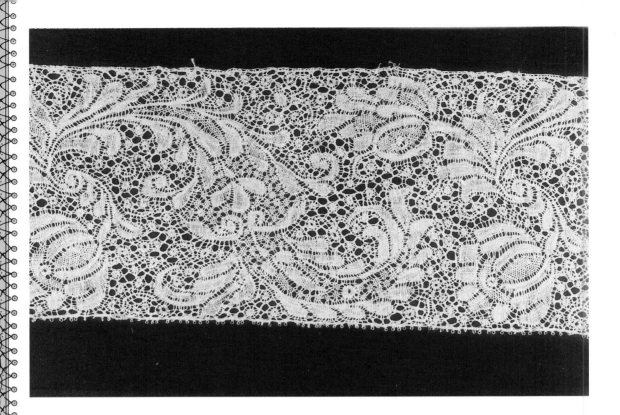

Above: Binche lace, actual size (6.5 cm)
Below: Detail of the above lace

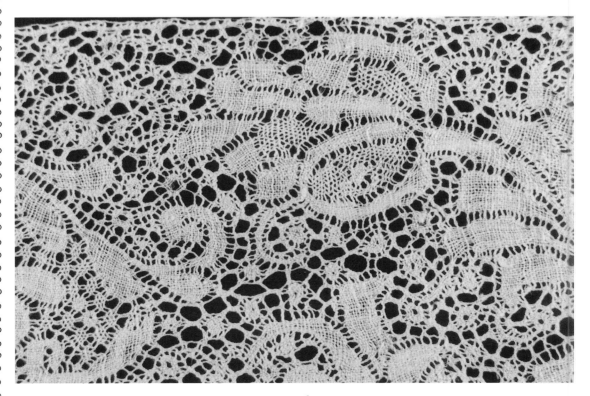

Above and below: Detail of the lace on the facing page

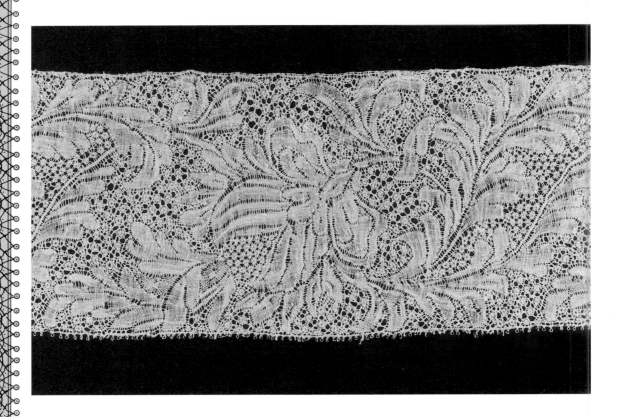

Above: Binche lace, actual size (7.1 cm)
Below: Detail of the above lace

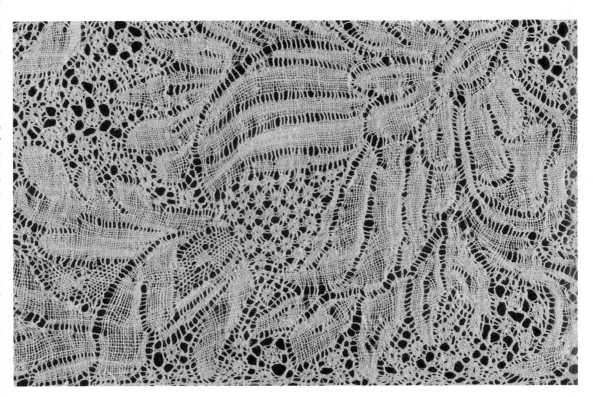

Above and below: Details of the lace on the facing page

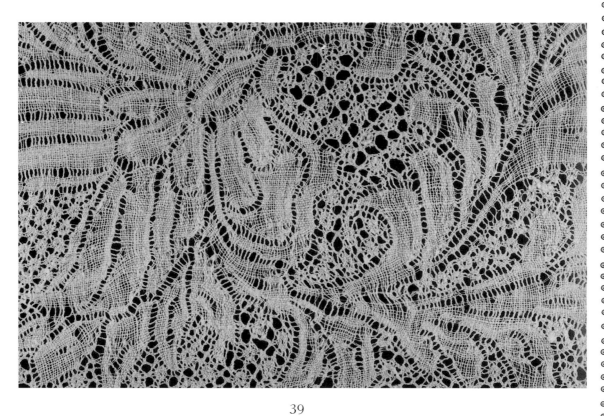

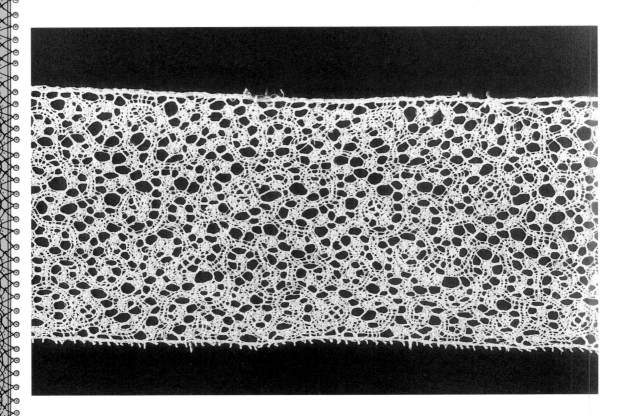

Above: Binche lace, actual size (6.2 cm)   **Below:** Detail of the above lace
Right: Binche prickings

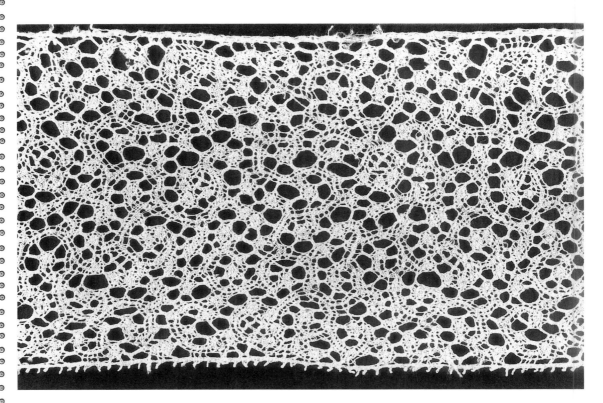

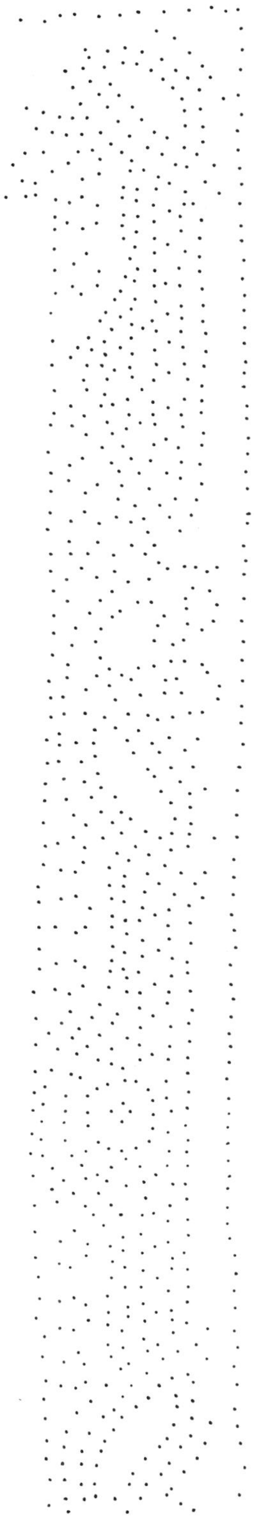
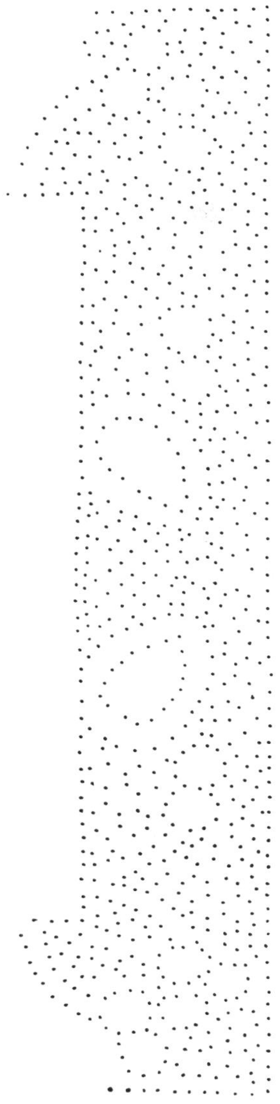
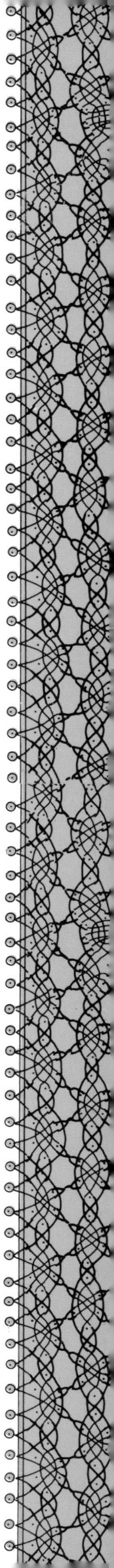

Right: Binche pricking; mentebolle work
Far right: Binche pricking; floral

Note on the snowflakes in Binche lace

Terminology creates many problems when describing the snowflakes of Binche. Terms such as 'fond de neige', 'oeil de perdrix' (Earnshaw '82), 'star' (Henneberg '31), 'holoed snowball' (Reigate '86). 'flocon de neige' (Van Steyvoort '82), 'snowflakes' and 'peas' (Verbeke-Billiet '85) have been used to describe them. This book uses the term 'snowflake' as a general all-encompassing term. The snowflakes given in this book have also been categorised into small, with holes, elongated, in frame or with ring.

Another problem is created by the terms 'ground' and 'filling'. The ground is the stitchwork which holds the design in place, and a filling fills an enclosed area of the design. Point de Paris, Valenciennes and Flanders lace all have their own distinct ground, as illustrated earlier, and all use snowflakes as fillings. In Binche lace, snowflakes may be used as fillings or as a ground. No distinction is made between the two, so that what may be a filling in Flanders lace might be a ground in Binche lace.

For each category there is a grid which is used to establish the correct proportion of each particular snowflake. The grid also illustrates how the pricking of the snowflakes is decided. The following sample pieces have been worked out on proportionally exact grids, but in many pieces of Binche lace these proportions and the placements of pinholes are changed to conform to the design of the lace. Snowflakes are often flattened or elongated slightly depending on the space or distance from the motif.

The connections of snowflakes to the footside or to the picot edge in the following sample pieces are all very regular, implying that they are worked consistently during the same piece. The connection of snowflakes to a motif may either be similar to, or very different from, the connections to the footside or to the picot edge. The following diagrams show some of the more common connections.

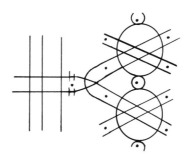

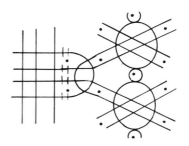

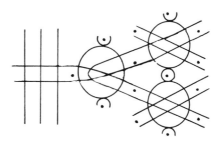

It will become evident upon working the various snowflakes that there are only four different grids given in this section, one for each of the following: small snowflake, snowflake, snowflake in a frame, and snowflake in a ring 1. Although there is only one grid for the snowflake, the grid has been altered at the picot edge to show different types of connection.

It is possible to place any of the snowflakes in half stitch, linen stitch, or with holes into the snowflakes in a ring or in a frame, and any small snowflake may be worked inside the snowflake in a ring 2.

Not only may the snowflakes inside the ring vary, but also the connections between them may be changed. Either a whole stitch or a small braid may be used.

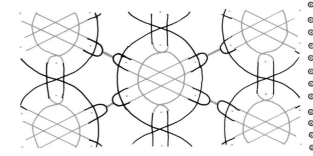

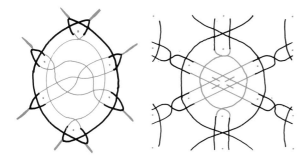

As a rule, snowflakes were not mixed in the same filling or ground, but occasionally one or two snowflakes of different types were used to enhance the design and to add interest.

The connections between the rings also have an alternative, often called a 'bridge'. The choice of which solution to use is up to the individual lacemaker.

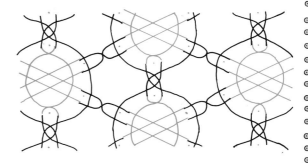

Although the following snowflakes have been worked out to be regular, in the majority of Binche laces this is not the case. When snowflakes take up a large area, most will be worked consistently. When snowflakes are scattered throughout the design, they will be worked as space allows. When working snowflakes with holes, some lacemakers use an additional pin in the centre of the snowflake to keep the hole open; other lacemakers do not. To assist the lacemaker when working the lace, a blue dot is drawn on the pricking to indicate a snowflake.

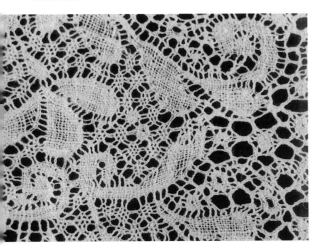

Note on the snowflake grids

The snowflakes of Binche also require unique grids to create the prickings. For the snowflakes presented in this section only three basic grids will need to be drawn. All grids, if being used to make the prickings, should be drawn on 2 mm graph paper. If you are working out diagrams, a much larger graph paper should be chosen.

The term 'unit', rather than a set measurement will be used in the following explanations to allow the lacemaker to construct these grids on whatever scale is preferred.

For the small snowflake grid, points are spaced one unit high by one unit wide. For connections with the edge, the points will need to be placed one unit apart and half a unit below the other pins.

The grids for snowflake in linen stitch, half stitch and with a hole are all the same. To draw this grid, the top horizontal line should be divided into units of two. The vertical sides should be divided into units of one.

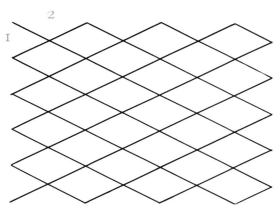

After the diagonals have been drawn, vertical lines will need to be added to divide the basic diamond in a 1:2:1 ratio. Black dots, indicating pin holes, are drawn at all points at which lines intersect.

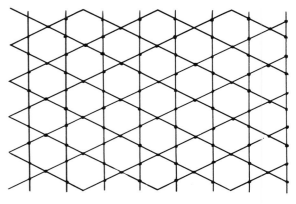

The various connections used in the snowflake samples are illustrated.

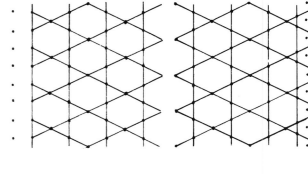

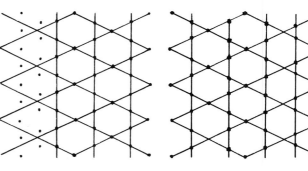

The grid for an elongated snowflake begins with the diamond grid explained above. The vertical lines need not be drawn. Elongated snowflakes each require a space three diamonds high. After the basic grid has been drawn, the outline for each snowflake should be marked. Two colours are used on the illustration to enable the lacemaker to see each more clearly. Pinholes are placed at the points at which the diamond grid crosses these outlines. The connection to the edge is also shown.

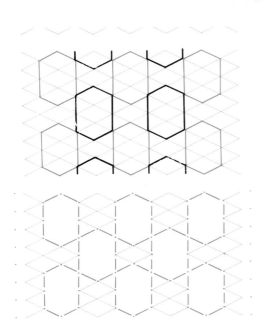

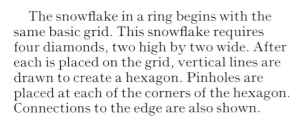

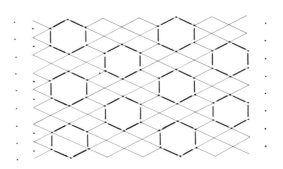

The grid for the snowflake in a frame requires a basic diamond four units wide by three units high. The outline for each snowflake requires four diamonds. Like the snowflake in a ring, a hexagon is drawn with pinholes at all corners. The spacing for the snowflake in a frame is different from the others, since space is needed for the 'frame'.

The snowflake in a ring begins with the same basic grid. This snowflake requires four diamonds, two high by two wide. After each is placed on the grid, vertical lines are drawn to create a hexagon. Pinholes are placed at each of the corners of the hexagon. Connections to the edge are also shown.

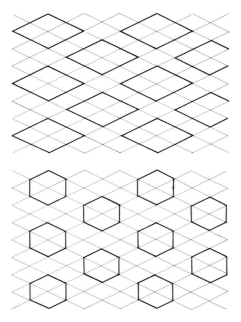

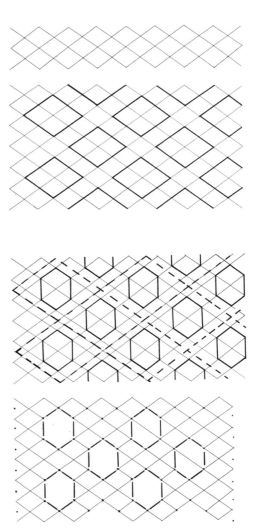

47

Small snowflakes

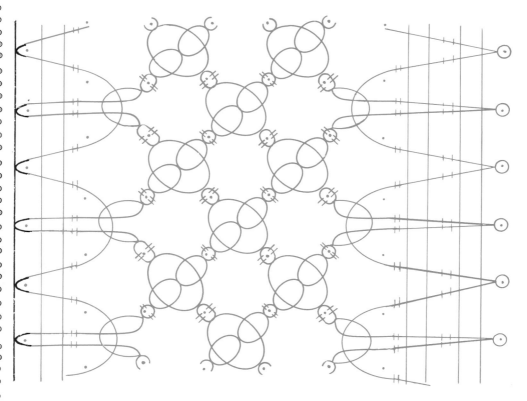

Above: Small snowflake 1 **Below left:** Pricking **Below right:** Photograph of small snowflake 1. Bobbins required: 34

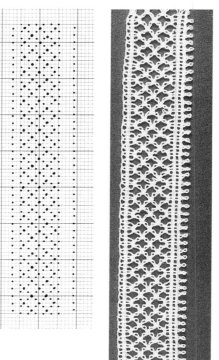

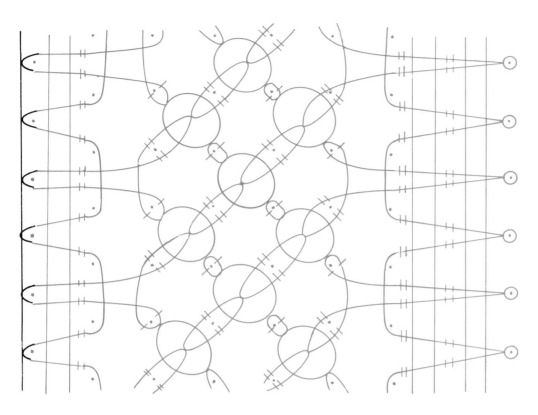

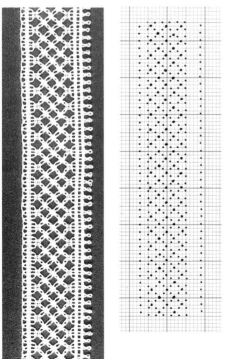

Above: Small snowflake 2 **Below left:** Photograph of small snowflake 2 **Below right:** Pricking. Bobbins required: 34

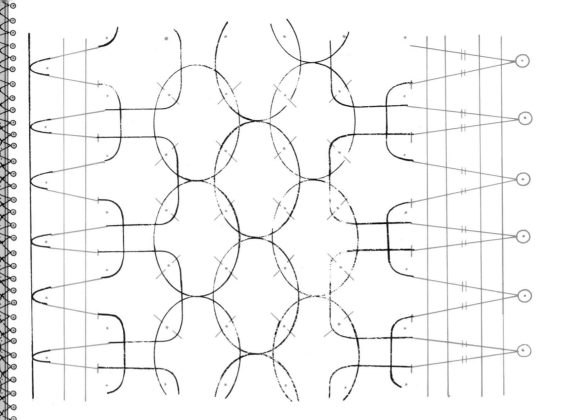

Above: Small snowflake 3   **Below left:**
Pricking   **below right:** Photograph of
small snowflake 3. Bobbins required: 34

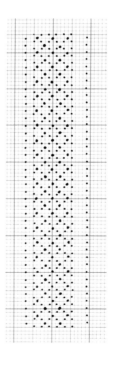

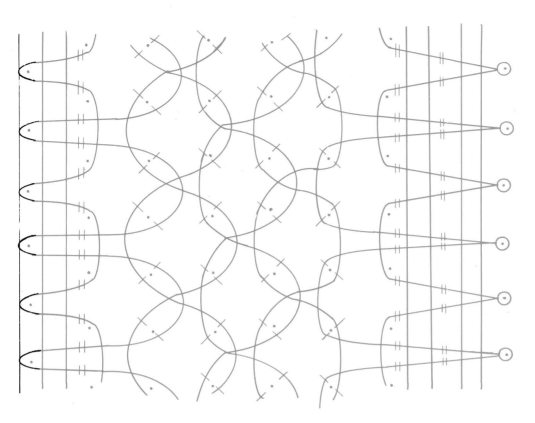

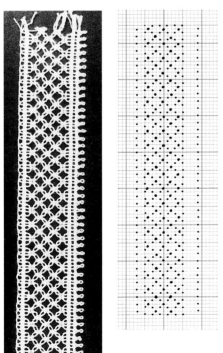

Above: Small snowflake 4   **Below left:**
Photograph of small snowflake 2   **Below
right:** Pricking. Bobbins required: 34

Snowflake in linen stitch

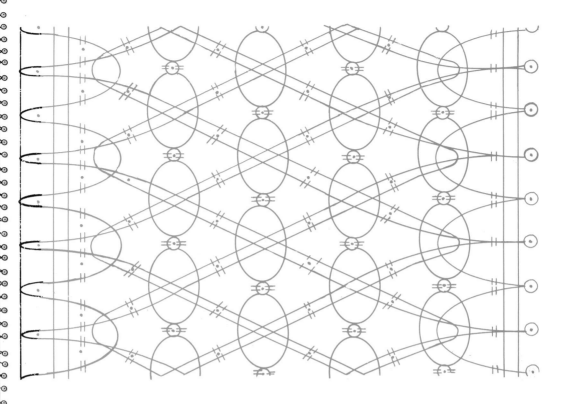

Above: Snowflake in linen stitch
Below left: Pricking   **Below right:**
Photograph of snowflake in linen. Bobbins
required: 46

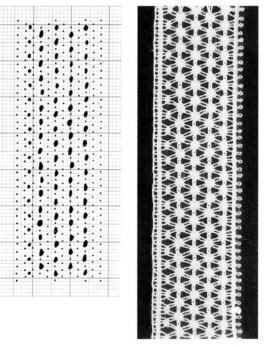

Snowflake in half stitch

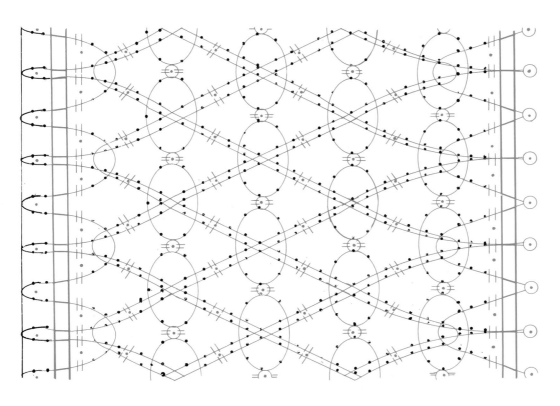

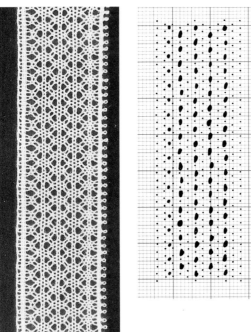

Above: Snowflake in half stitch   **Below left:** Photograph of snowflake in half stitch   **Below right:** Pricking. Bobbins required: 46

Snowflake with hole: 1

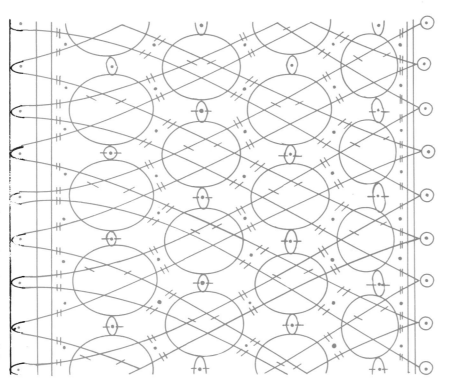

Above: Snowflake with hole 1   **Below:** (from left to right) Pricking, snowflake with hole 1, snowflake with hole 2, snowflake with hole 2. Bobbins required: 42

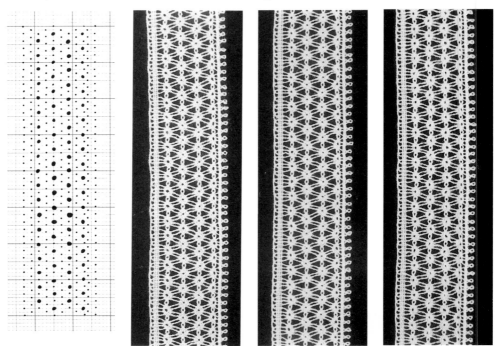

Snowflake with hole: 2 & 3

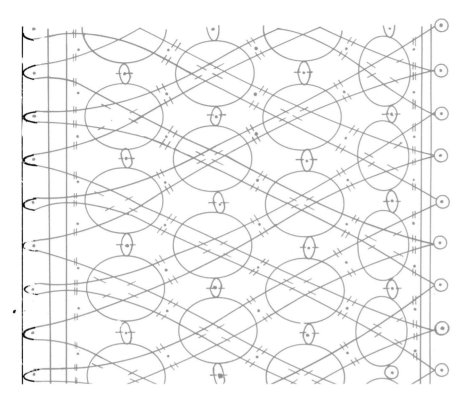

Above: Snowflake with hole 2   **Below:** Snowflake with hole 3

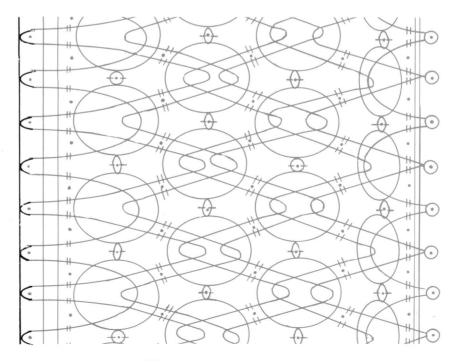

Snowflake with hole: 4

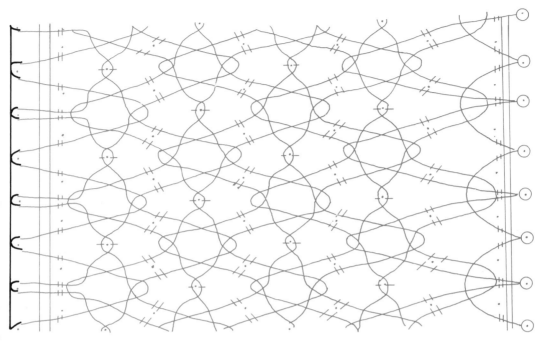

Above: Snowflake with hole 4 **Below:** (from left to right) Pricking, snowflake with hole 4, snowflake with hole 5, snowflake with hole 6. Bobbins required: 42

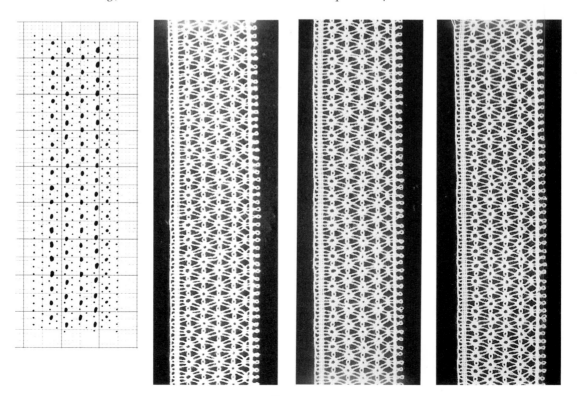

Snowflake with hole: 5 & 6

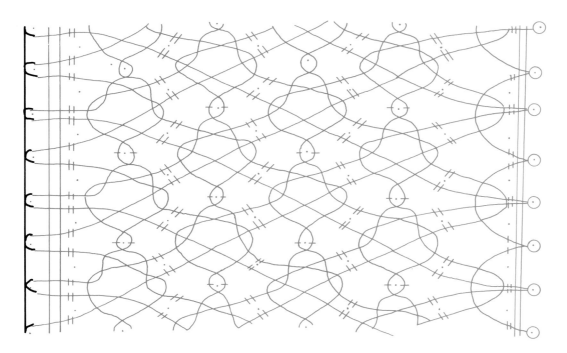

Above: Snowflake with hole 5
Below: Snowflake with hole 6

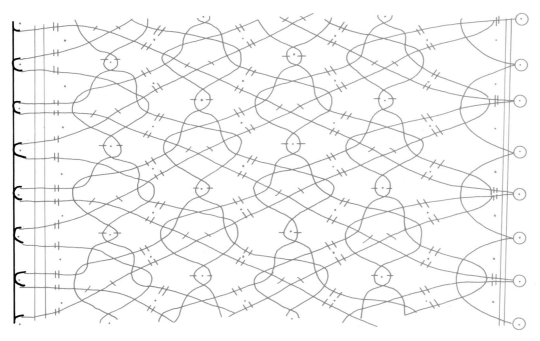

Elongated snowflake

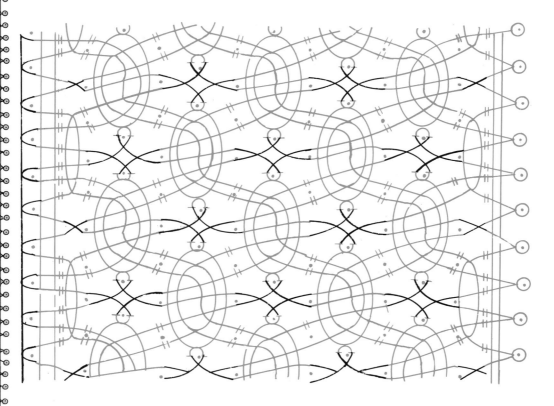

Above: Elongated snowflake 1 **Below left:** Pricking **Below right:** Photograph of elongated snowflake 1. Bobbins required: 58

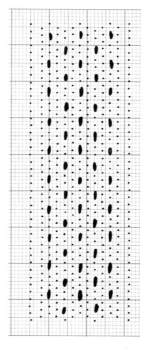

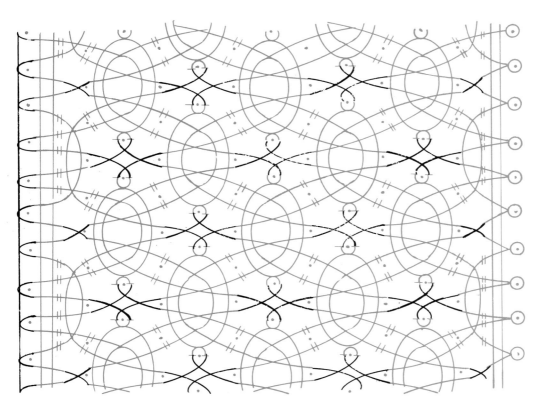

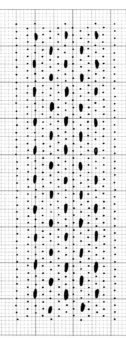

Above and below left: Elongated
snowflake 2 **Below right:** Pricking.
Bobbins required: 58

Snowflake in a frame

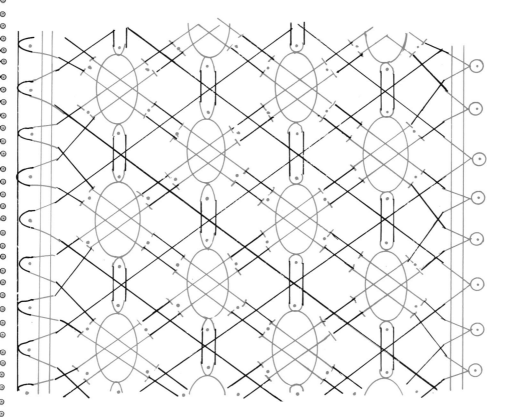

Above: Snowflake in a frame **Below left:**
Pricking **Below right:** Snowflake in a
frame. Bobbins required: 56

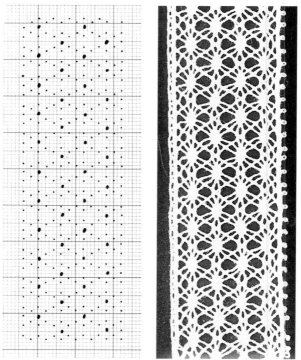

Snowflake in a ring: 1

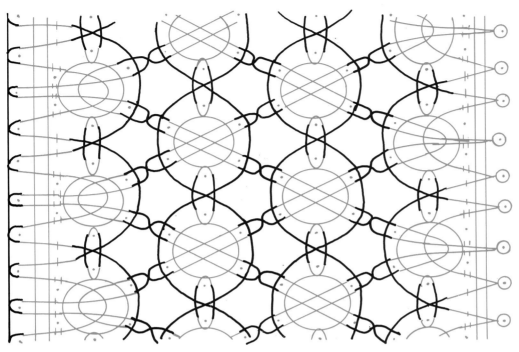

Above and below left: Snowflake in a ring 1. **Below right:** Pricking. Bobbins required: 54

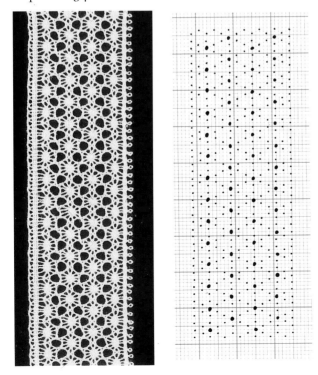

Snowflake in a ring: 2

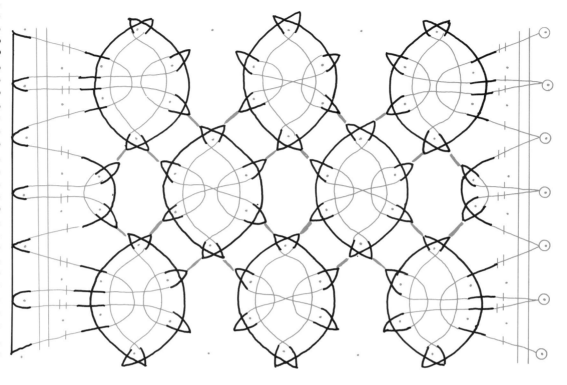

Above: Snowflake in a ring 2   **Below left:** Pricking   **Below right:** Snowflake in a ring 2.
Bobbins required: 54

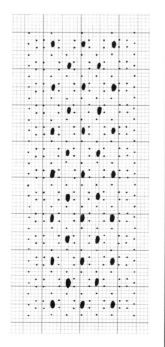

Snowflake in a ring: 3

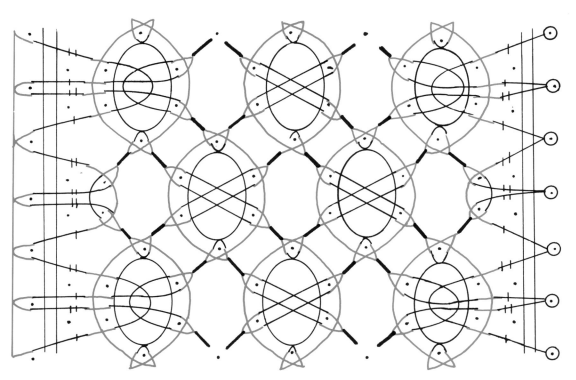

Above and below left: Snowflake in a ring 3
Below right: Pricking. Bobbins required: 54

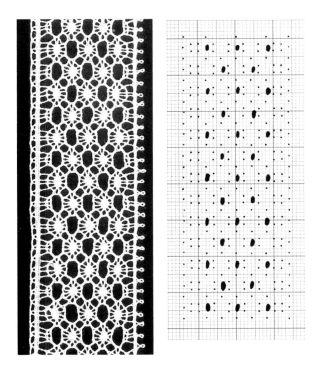

Note on bookmarks

The following prickings are for three exercises in working snowflakes. They have been included at the end of this section to give the lacemaker practice in the various snowflakes and the opportunity to create a 'finished' piece, as opposed to a simple sample.

These pieces are not true examples of Binche lace: they are just snowflakes. True Binche lace usually has a picot edge (worked on the right) and a sewing edge (worked on the left). The exception to this is a Binche insertion, which will have a sewing edge on both the right and the left sides. To give the bookmark a symmetrical appearance, a picot edge is needed on both sides.

There are two ways of finishing the bookmark. The first, which is the easiest, is to carry all the extra passive pairs as a bundle along the inside of the passive pairs used for the picot edge. To accomplish this, first work the inside pair from the snowflake out to complete the picot. Then work the pair back through the passive pairs. This process is continued until there are enough passive pairs to pass as a bundle, as opposed to working them in linen stitch. Remember that you always keep the outside two pairs as passives for the picot edge; they should not be included in the passive bundle.

The second method for finishing the bookmark is to end the pairs at the picot. This is similar to starting pairs at the picot. The process is as follows: work the inside pair from the snowflake out through the passive pairs and complete the picot. Stop. Take the other pair from the snowflake and work it through the passive pairs. Place this pair to the side or to the back of the pillow, somewhere where it cannot be used again. Then take the pair that completed the picot and work it back through the three passive pairs. The pair is then placed to the side or to the back of the pillow, where it cannot be used again. This process is then repeated for the next picot.

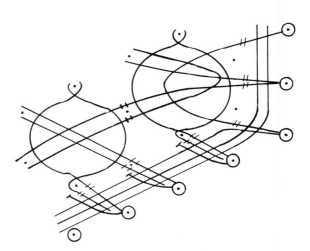

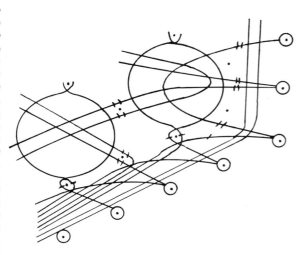

Bookmark 1

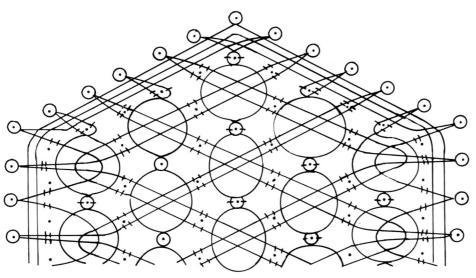

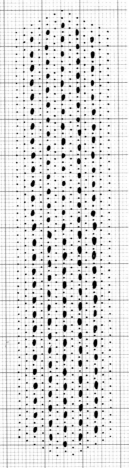

Above and below: Bookmark 1
Bottom: Pricking. Bobbins required: 48

Bookmark 2

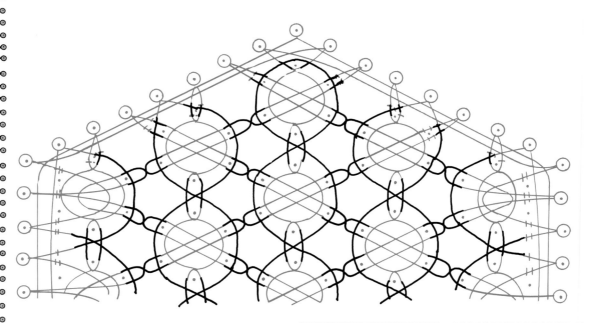

Above and below: Bookmark 2
Bottom: Pricking. Bobbins required: 64

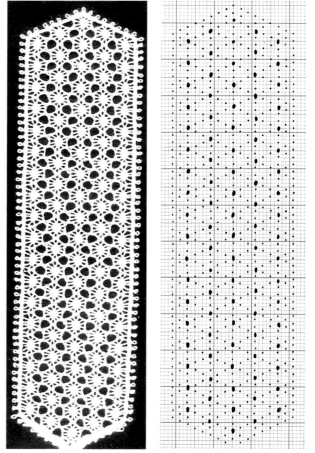

Bookmark 3

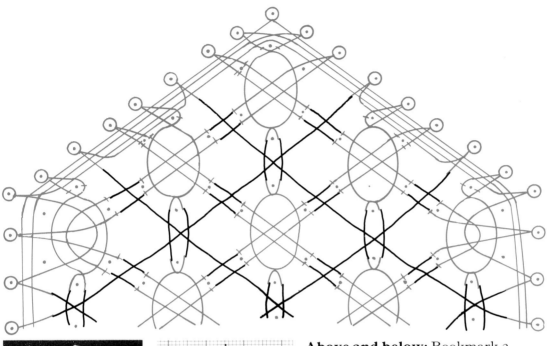

Above and below: Bookmark 3
Bottom: Pricking. Bobbins required: 56

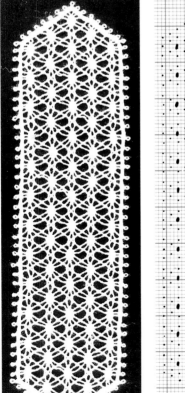

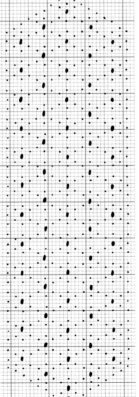

Note on patterns

Introduction

The patterns included in this section are for a variety of Binche laces. Starting with the brick and continuing through Binche with tallies, these patterns utilise the techniques already explained. The following additional notes should assist the lacemaker.

Threads

A variety of thread sizes may be used in working Binche lace. A coarse pattern, such as the large mentebolle, may use a 70 cotton. There are a number of very fine patterns which require 180 cotton. The spectrum of thread sizes is vast. The lacemaker's preference plays an important role in the thread selection. Some lacemakers who prefer a heavier, tighter lace will chose a thicker thread. To achieve a much lighter, open lace a thinner thread should be used.

The thread size given with each pattern is the size with which the piece was worked. This should be used as a guide only.

Prickings

The prickings used for Binche lace have a series of markings to indicate to the lacemaker how the piece should be worked. Snowflakes are indicated by a black circle, a black dot or lines outlining the pinholes of the snowflake.

To indicate half stitch a cross hatch is drawn on the pricking. In the following patterns, half stitch is shown on the pricking, but not on the diagram.

Bricks 1 and 2

Thread: 100/3 Brok cotton   Bobbins: 46

Bricks 1 and 2 are based on the traditional pattern of the same name. Brick 1 is the closest in appearance to the original, although the original was worked straight, not in the round. Both are simple patterns, using only snowflake in a ring and linen stitch.

Binche with Valenciennes ground

This piece uses Valenciennes ground between each motif. In Binche lace the Valenciennes ground seen most often is the diamond mesh. The round mesh appears only in pieces worked in the round, where the round mesh adapts to the curve better than the diamond mesh. When Valenciennes ground is used in Binche lace, the length of the braid varies, depending upon need.

Below is the repeat used to lengthen the size of the pattern. The pattern is reversible: either side may serve as the picot edge.

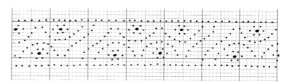

Sideways three

Thread: 120 Egyptian cotton
Bobbins: 42

The original diagram for this piece comes from *Bedrijfsleer de Kanten*, a teaching manual published in 1916. The traditional piece was worked straight.

Abstract design

Thread: 170 Chain Coats cotton
Bobbins: 54

This piece is similar to the antique piece on page 79. To be a true reproduction of the antique lace, the working diagram should be changed to the one below. The decision to work the outside pair in whole stitch was that of the author.

Small mentebolle

Thread: 140 Egyptian cotton
Bobbins: 44

This is another piece which offers a mixture of stitch work. Paris ground, half stitch, linen stitch, snowflakes in linen and snowflake in a ring are used in this lace. This piece also illustrates different connections of the snowflake in a ring to the picot edge. The necessity of taking pairs out on one side and replacing them on the other is also shown.

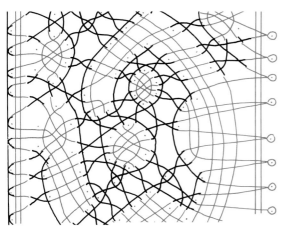

Mentebolle

Thread: 120 Egyptian cotton
Bobbins: 70

A rather clean design with no really complex stitch work. This piece does offer the opportunity to make some unusual take-ins and take-outs.

Large Mentebolle

Thread: 70 Egyptian cotton
Bobbins: 180

This is a straightforward piece. It is made up of a number of different stitches: snowflake in linen, snowflake in a ring with connecting braids, Paris ground, half stitch and linen stitch.

The challenge in this piece lies in managing the 180 bobbins.

Binche with tallies

Thread: 120 Egyptian cotton
Bobbins: 62

This piece offers the lacemaker to work not only small snowflakes but also tallies. The small snowflakes are very easy to work, whereas many lacemakers find tallies a bother. The lacemaker should be aware that two different ways of working a tally are used in this piece. Pairs not only hang down from one pin but also from two different pins. On the diagrams tallies are indicated by blue lines (see below).

Brick 1

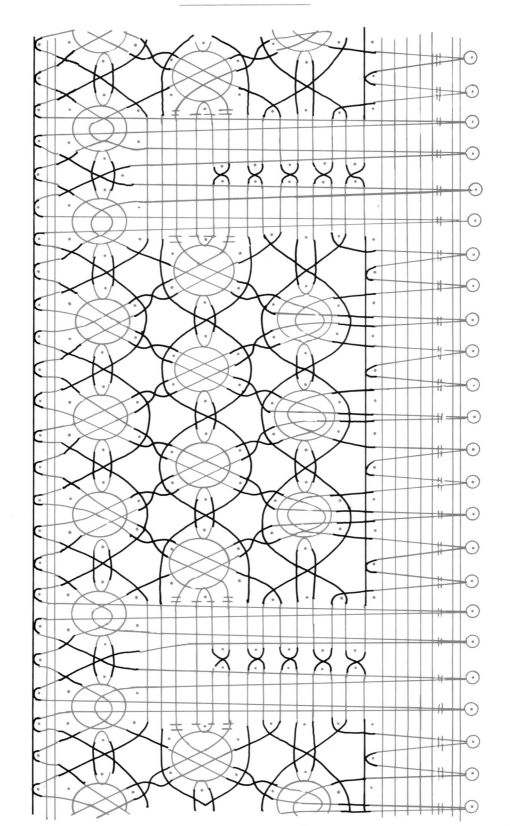

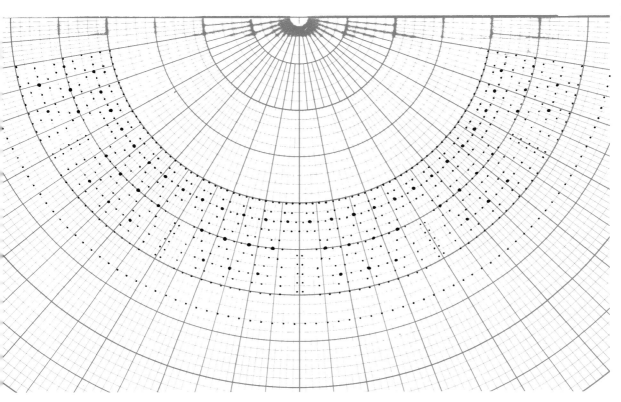

Left: Brick 1   **Above:** Pricking   **Below:** Brick 1. Bobbins required: 58

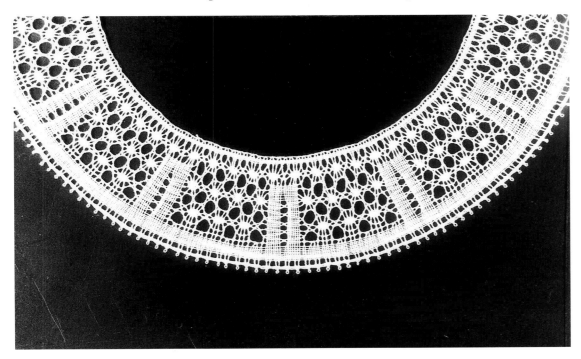

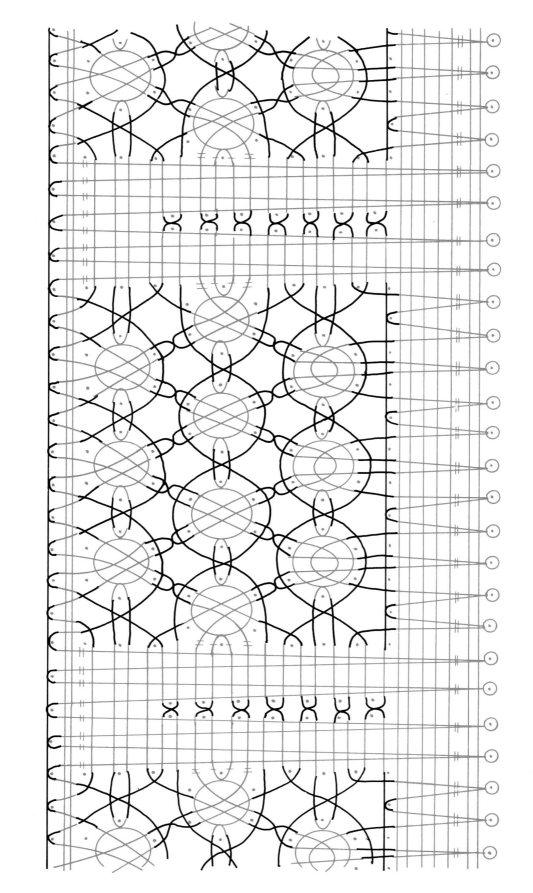

Brick 2

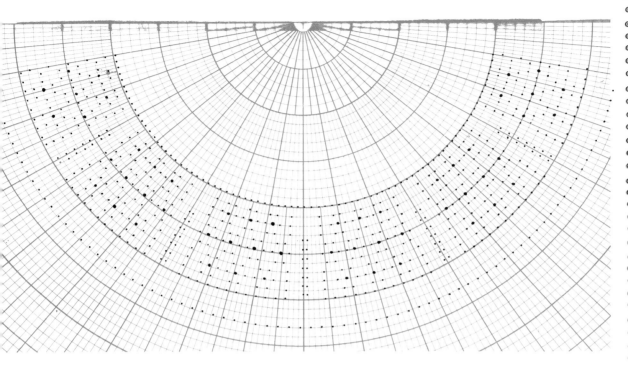

Left: Brick 2   **Above:** Pricking   **Below:** Brick 2. Bobbins required: 58

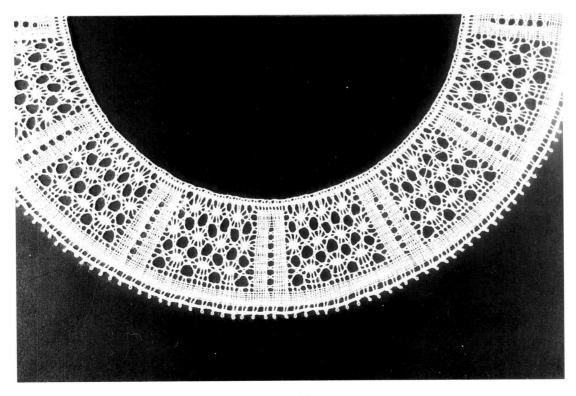

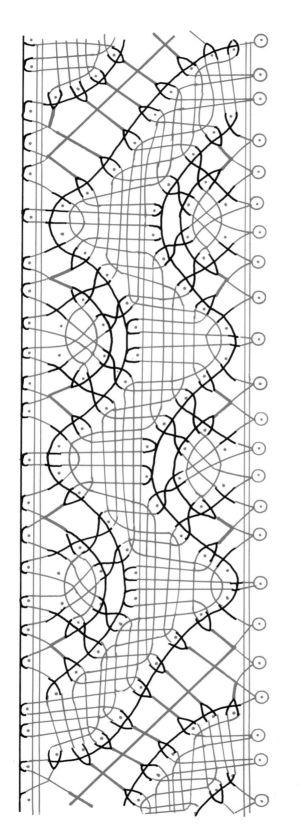
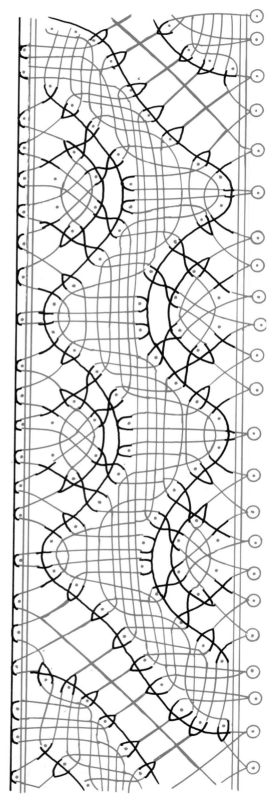

Binche with Valenciennes ground

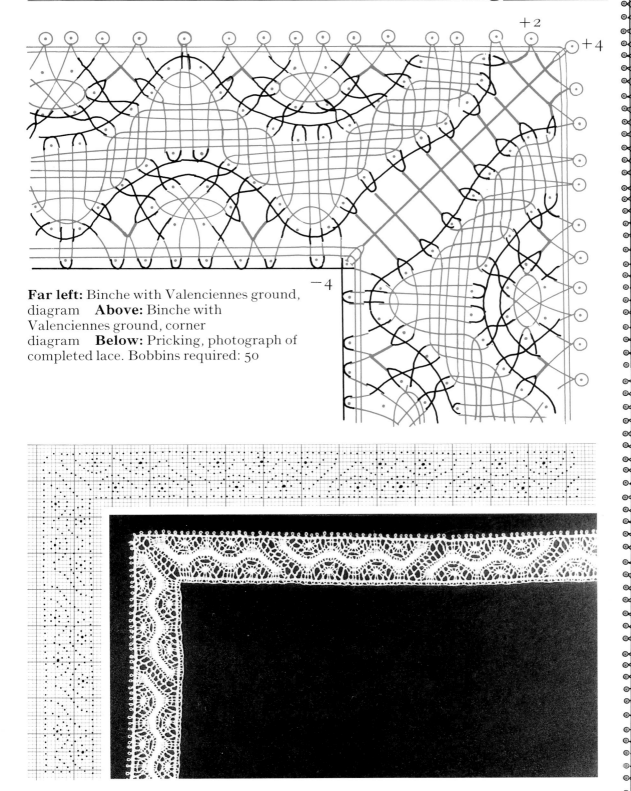

+2
+4
−4

Far left: Binche with Valenciennes ground, diagram **Above:** Binche with Valenciennes ground, corner diagram **Below:** Pricking, photograph of completed lace. Bobbins required: 50

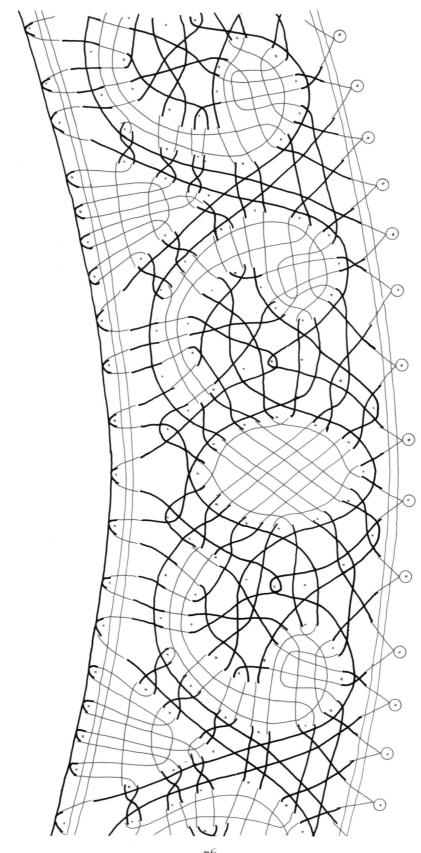

Sideways three

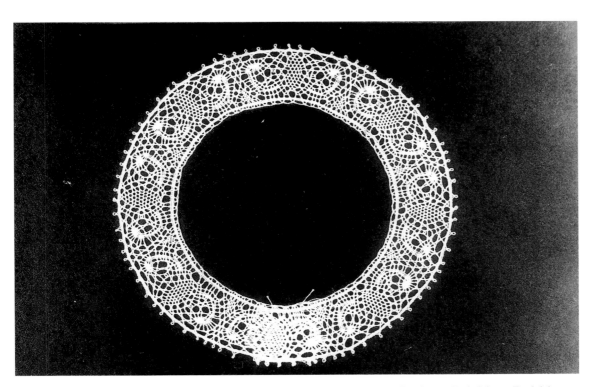

Far left: Sideways three diagram **Above:** Sideways three **Below:** Pricking. Bobbins
required: 40

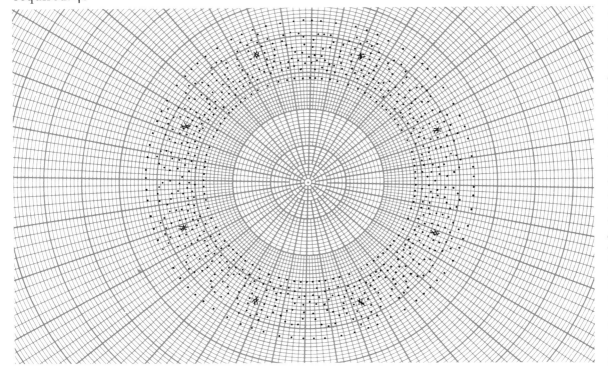

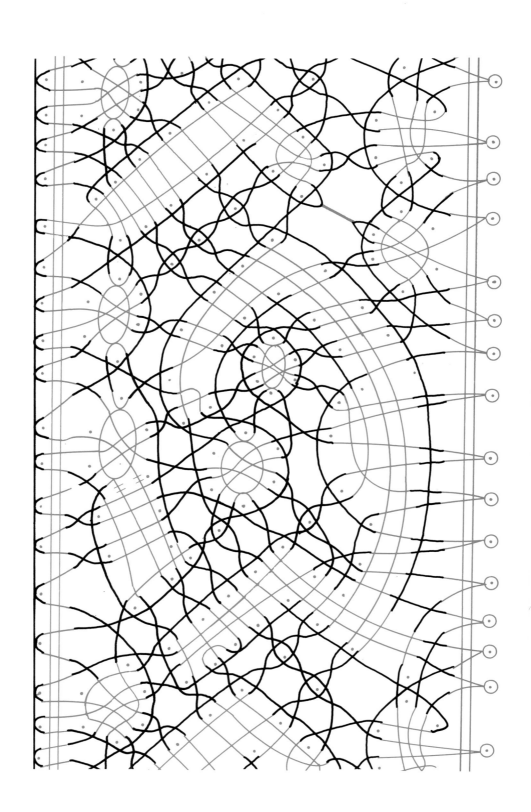

Abstract design

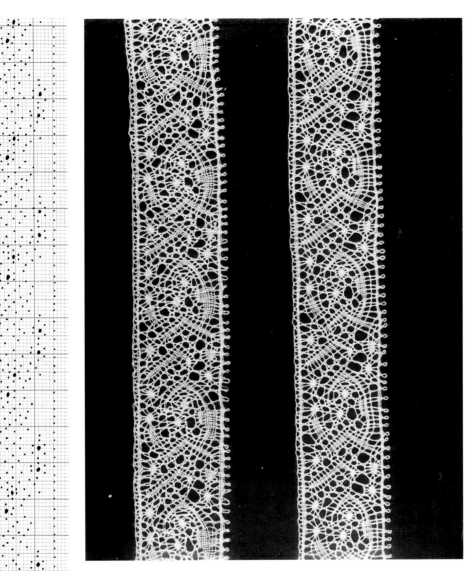

Far left: Abstract design   **Left:** Pricking   **Above:** (from left to right) Original antique lace; contemporary version. Bobbins required: 54

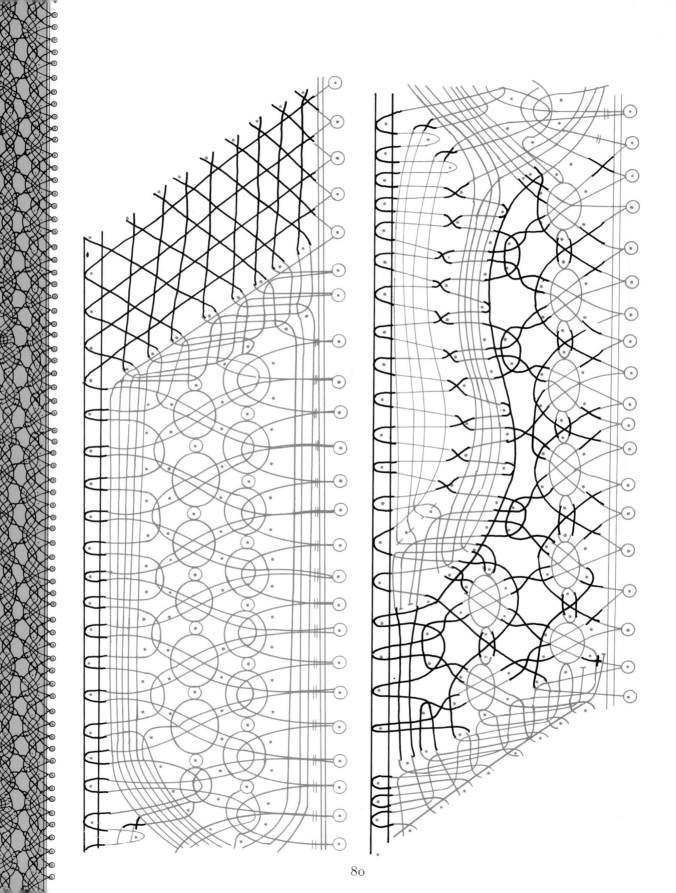

Small mentebolle

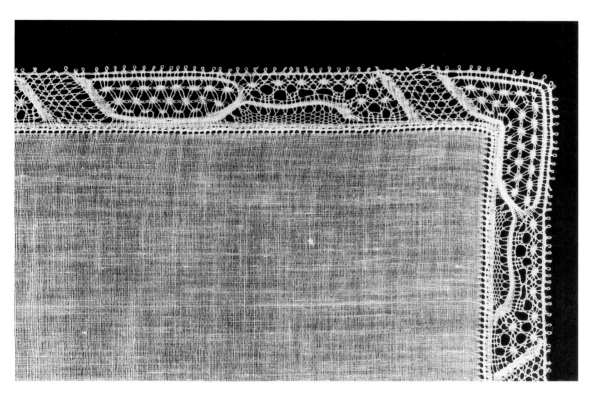

Left: Small mentebolle, diagram   **Above:** Small mentebolle   **Below:** Pricking. Bobbins required: 44

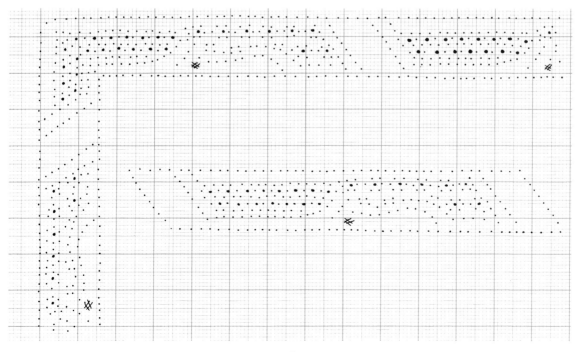

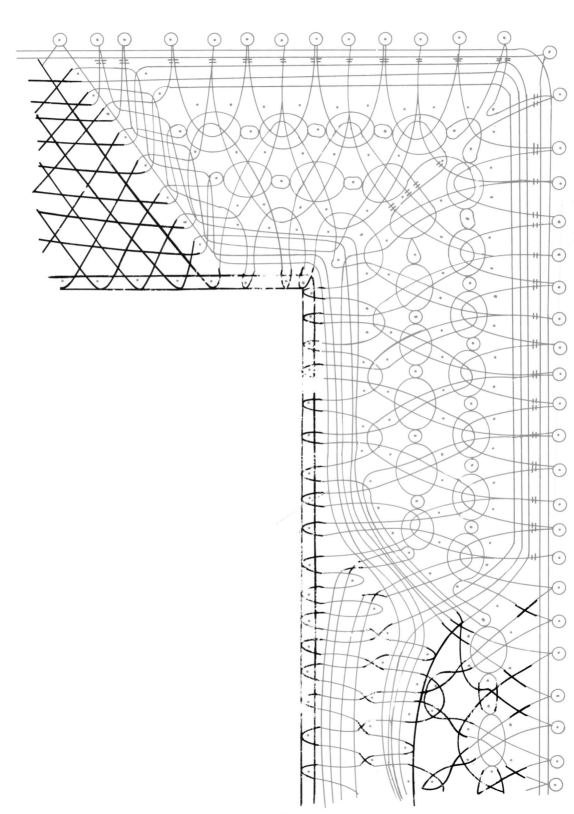

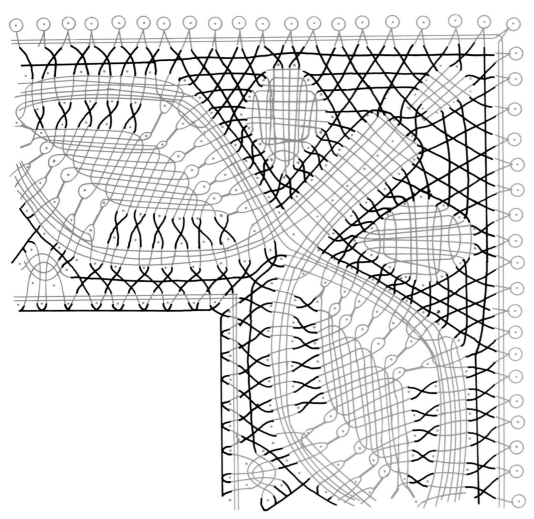

Left: Small mentebolle, corner diagram
Above: Mentebolle, corner diagram

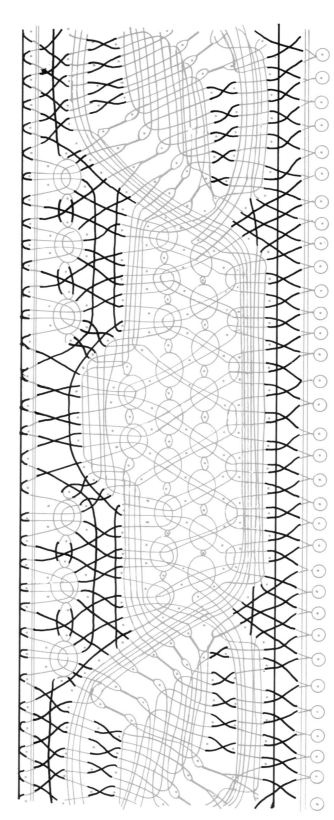

Mentebolle

Left: Mentebolle, diagram   **Above:** Mentebolle
Below: Pricking. Bobbins required: 70

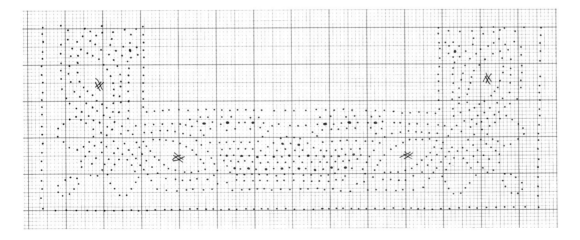

Large mentebolle

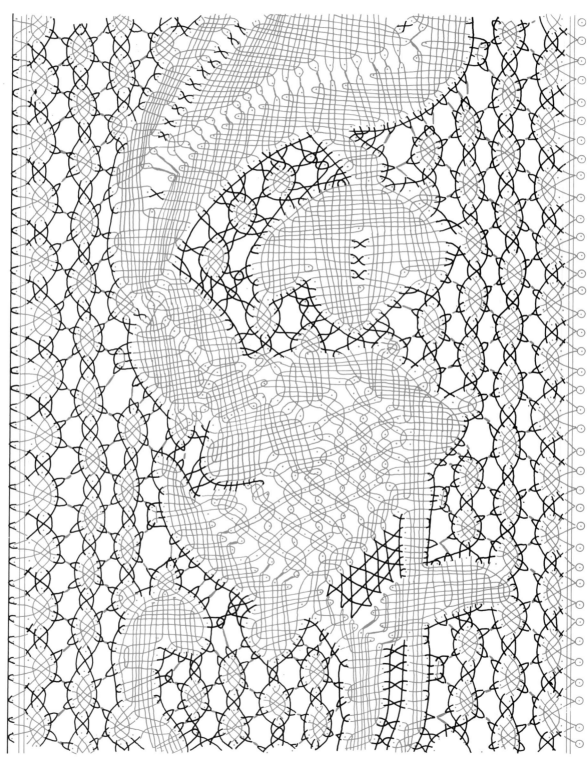

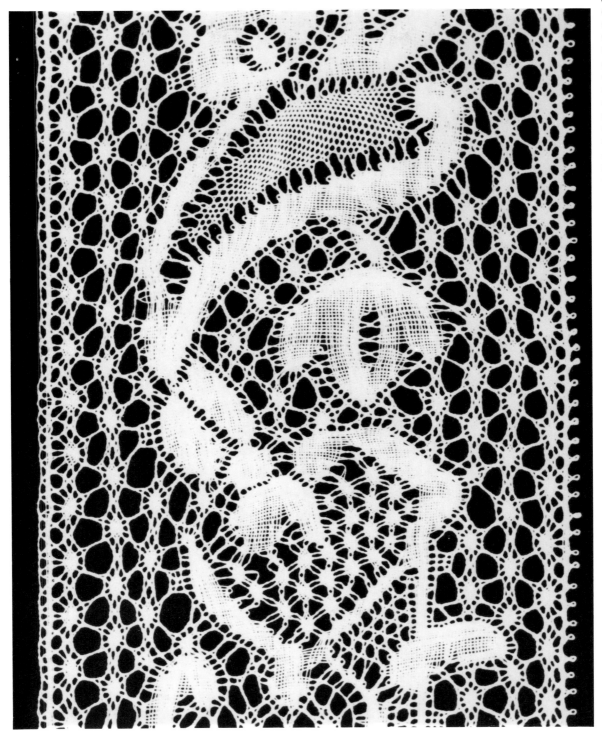

Left: Large mentebolle, diagram   **Above:** Large mentebolle. Bobbins required: 180

Above: Large mentebolle, diagram   **Right:** Pricking

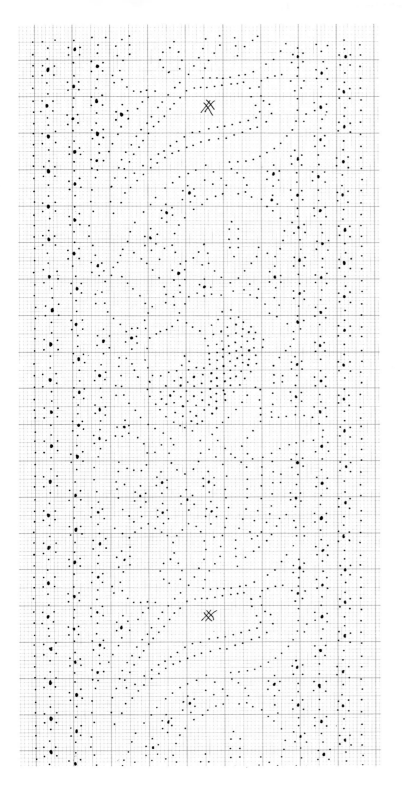

Binche with tallies

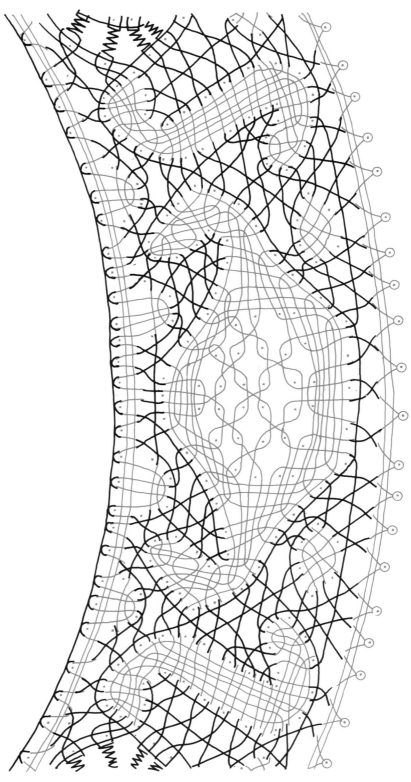

Far left: Binche with tallies, diagram   **Above:** Binche with tallies. Bobbins required: 62

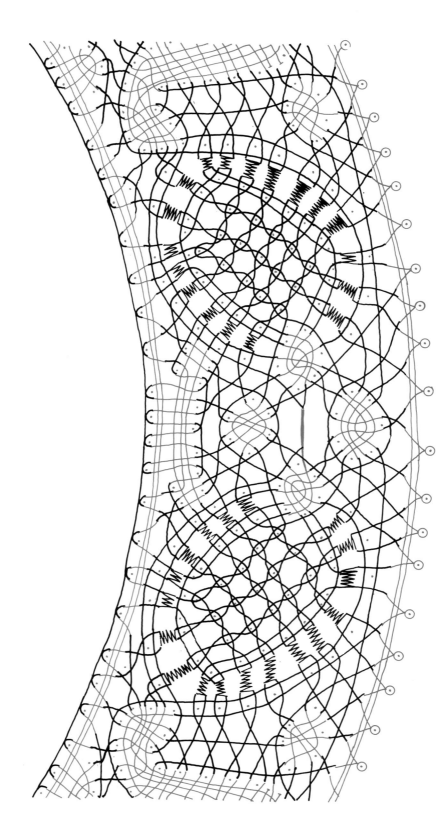

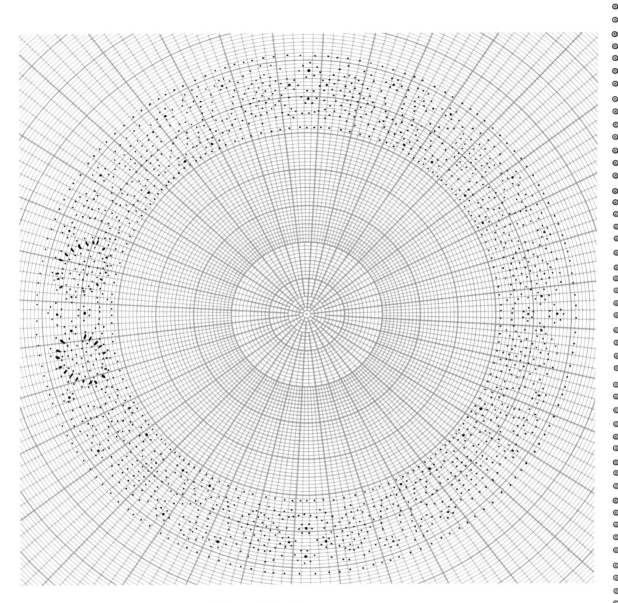

Far left: Binche with tallies   **Above:** Pricking

Further reading

Blum, Clara, *Old World Lace*, New York, 1920

Carlier de Lantsheeve, Antoine, *Les Dentelles a la Main*, Paris, 1906

Carlier de Lantsheeve, Antoine, *Tresor de l'art Dentellier*, Paris, 1922

Earnshaw, Pat, *A Dictionary of Lace*, London, 1982

Earnshaw, Pat, *The Identification of Lace*, London, 1980

Henneberg, Alfred von, *The Art & Craft of Old Lace*, London, 1931

Jones, Maty Eirwen, *The Romance of Lace*, London, 1951

Jourdain, M., *Old Lace: A Handbook for Collectors*, London, 1908 (reprinted 1988)

Pollen, Mrs John Hungerford, *Seven Centuries of Lace*, New York, 1908

Reigate, Emily, *An Illustrated Guide to Lace*, Woodbridge, 1986

Roberts, Edna, *How to Know Laces*, New York, 1925

Schutte, Marie, *Alt Spitzen*, Berlin, 1926

Simeon, Margaret, *The History of Lace*, London, 1979

Stuckens, Irene, *Bedrijfsleer der Kanten*, Brugge, 1916

Vandoren, B., *De Binske Kant of Binche Apostoline Specialiteit* (unpublished)

Van Steyvoort, Colette, *Initation à la Création Dentelliere*, Paris, 1982

Verbeke-Billiet, Annamarie, *Syllabus: Binche I*, Brugge, 1985

Suppliers

BELGIUM
Textiel Scharlaeken
Philipstockstraat 5–7
B–800 Brugge

Marc DeMaertelaere
Hooistraat 124
9210 Destelbergen-
Heusden

T'Handwerkjuisje
Katelinjnestraat 23
B–8000 Brugge

Willy Baetsle
Ten Berg 49
B–9300   Aalst

GERMANY
Brigitte Wichlei
Der Fenster-Laden
Berliner Strasse 8
6483 Bad Soden-
Salmunster

ENGLAND
Alby Lace Centre
Cromer Road
Alby
Norwich
Norfolk

Frank Herring & Sons
27 High West Street
Dorchester
DT1 1UP

Loricraft
4 Big Lane
Lambourn
Berks RG16 7XQ

Honiton Lace Shop
44 High Street
Honiton
Devon

Mace and Nairn
89 Crane Street
Salisbury
Wilts

The Lace Guild
The Hollies
53 Audnam
Stourbridge
West Midlands
DY8 4AE

D. H. Shaw
47 Zamor Crescent
Thurscroft
Rotherham
South Yorks

John & Jennifer Ford
October Hill
Upper Way
Upper Longdon
Rugeley
Staffs WS15 1QB

Shireburn Lace
Finkle Court
Finkle
Serburn in Elmet
North Yorks

Enid Taylor
Valley House Craft
Studio
Ruston
Scarborough
North Yorks
YO13 9QE

George White
Delaheys Cottage
Thistle Hill
Knaresborough
North Yorks

English Lace School
Oak House
Church Stile
Woodbury
near Exeter
Devon

D. J. Hornsby
149 High Street
Burton Latimer
Kettering
Northants
NN15 5RL

Liz Bartlett
12 Creslow Court
Galley Hill
Stony Stratford
MK11 1NN

Seblace
Waterloo Mill
Howden Road
Silsden
West Yorks BD20 0HA

T. Brown
Woodside
Greenlands Lane
Prestwood
Great Missenden
Bucks

A. Sells
49 Pedley Lane
Clifton
Shefford
Beds

C. & D. Springett
21 Hillmorton Road
Rugby
Warks CV22 5DF

B. Phillips
Pantglas
Cellen
Lampeter
Dyfed

Newnham Lace
Equipment
11 Dorcheser Close
Basingstoke
Hants RG23 8EX

Bartlett, Caeser &
Partners
The Glen
Downton
Lymington
Hants

95

UNITED STATES

Lacis
2990 Adeline Street
Berkeley, California
94703

Robin & Russ
Handweavers
533 North Adams
Street
McMinnville, Oregon
97128

Van Siever Bobbin Lace
130 Cascadilla Park
Ithaca, New York
14850